Between the Microwave and the Mall

FINDING GOD IN EVERYDAY PLACES

✻

Merilyn Packer

First edition published March 2004 by Openbook Publishers
Second edition (v2.1) published August 2009 by Luminant Publications

Luminant Publications
PO Box 305
Greenacres SA 5085
Australia

https://www.ozpacker.com/merilynpacker

National Library of Australia
Cataloguing-in-Publication entry
Packer, Merilyn Denise.
Between the microwave and the mall : finding God in everyday places.

ISBN 978-0-9806963-0-1

Cover Design by Karyn Edwards

ABOUT THE AUTHOR

Merilyn Packer grew up in Adelaide, South Australia, and lives there with her husband Allan. Having successfully navigated their teenage years, all four of their children have now married. The grandchildren count is steadily growing.

After graduating from Adelaide and Flinders Universities, Merilyn worked as a clinical psychologist before travelling overseas and living in the UK for two years. Since then the family lived in northern California for several years before returning to Australia.

She is actively involved in church life and is regularly invited to speak at women's functions. She has also been involved in local schools ministry and focussed prayer initiatives of various kinds.

In addition to her long-standing column in *Christian Woman* magazine, Merilyn's writing has appeared in several books from the award-winning *Australian Stories* series by Strand Publishing.

PREFACE TO THE FIRST EDITION

Since 1993 I have had the joy and struggle of writing a column for the magazine *Christian Woman*. At first the column was titled 'Feelings', and I shared perspectives on handling difficult emotions. I felt a degree of responsibility since I carried a 'clinical psychologist' tag.

After three years I lost interest in the narrow focus on difficulties. The editor at *Christian Woman*, Sanna Wilson, kindly allowed me to branch out, and the column became 'Family Matters'. As I relaxed into writing more personally, the column flowed and became a pleasure to write. Over the years various commissioned articles complemented the column.

I revisited the articles after John Pfitzner and the team at Openbook accepted them for publication. It was satisfying to relive my last ten years of mothering as I began pruning and reshaping the material. When I began the column, my four children were aged 4 to 9. Now they are 14 to 19.

In regrouping the articles around themes, I haven't kept them in their chronological order; I trust the reader will not be confused as a result. A number of the 'Feelings and Passions' pieces have been reworked, and some of my attempts at poetry have been included to add variety.

I have greatly appreciated the encouragement of Sanna Wilson and her successor, Jenny Baxter. How do these women, with their families and busy lives, manage to edit magazines?

Thank you to John Pfitzner for your positive, gentle encouragement. A very big thankyou to my friends, and to my children, James, Melanie, Stephen and Deborah, for allowing me to lay our lives bare.

And, most of all, thank you to my husband and best friend, Allan. I would have given up writing the column years ago if he hadn't kept me to it, and I would never have got around to attempting publication. Allan's vision, initiative and work in finding, formatting and arranging the material has brought this about. Thank you.

March 2004

PREFACE TO THE SECOND EDITION

The 20th birthday of our youngest child last week confirms that I have moved on from the season recorded in these pages. I lit her birthday candles and high-fived my husband. We have survived four teenagers! It's done.

Skimming the pieces in this book brings the daily flavour of the last 20 years vividly before me. It's great to have a record of those precious times. With one child now married and at least the theoretical prospect of grandchildren before me, I don't want to forget the unique griefs, struggles and gold nuggets of family life with young children.

Five years have passed since the first edition was published and my husband has been gently but persistently reminding me that the intervening season is worth celebrating, too. Neither of us wants to forget the special joys and challenges of life with teenagers and emerging young adults.

The ongoing column in *Christian Woman* has been steadily chronicling the ups and downs of a stage of life that, for us at least, is now drawing to an end. Yet as I progress through life, I find myself encountering similar issues in different guises. Even as our children leave childhood behind, our parents become increasingly dependent. Life consists of seasons, and over time these seasons cycle around again and again as we age and our children grow up.

With all that in mind, another slim volume to follow up on this one may well be in order. Any news about a sequel will be posted on the book website at https://www.ozpacker.com/merilynpacker.

Meanwhile, I have been encouraged by the feedback from a new audience of women who have discovered this book through older friends. I trust this reprinted edition will bring a smile and some encouragement to those who weren't mothers when the first edition was published but are in the thick of it now. I'm cheering for you!

August 2009

BENDING WITHOUT BREAKING:
COPING WITH STRESS

ONE OF THOSE DAYS

One Friday afternoon recently I kissed my husband goodbye as he left on a weekend men's retreat. With the men away, a couple of new friends had suggested getting together. It seemed like a good opportunity.

Friday night I cooked a meal for one of them. The evening went smoothly if you don't count my uncontrollable urge to yawn whenever I sat still. Saturday morning I woke up tired. At ice-skating lessons when I agreed to let my girls invite two friends back for lunch, I forgot my husband had the minivan. So the friends' father had to come back to drive them to our house. With him following me I could hardly stop at the supermarket to buy those few essential items for Saturday night's dinner.

The other friend arrived shortly after the two girls left. Her four children plus my four soon became unmanageable in a small house. The solution was to head for the park. There the boys could pursue their new pleasure—roller-blading.

But our 10-year-old daughter didn't want to go to the park. With impressive drama she argued her point relentlessly: there was every reason in the world not to go; I was totally unfair; I always favour the other children.

Every parent knows these struggles are part of the fabric of life and need to be dealt with squarely whatever the circumstance.

Nevertheless an audience adds to the stress level - in this case eight wide-eyed onlookers.

The trip to the park was a qualified success. Detailed negotiation about sharing the rollerblades consumed much of the time. And have you noticed how there are never enough swings in parks?

To streamline, I'd prepared dinner in advance. When I served it the children were horrified. "Oh, no! Not THIS!" I hadn't made it to the supermarket to buy an alternative, so too bad. But the grizzle gauge hit an all-time high. By the time my friend and her children left I felt like a squeezed-out rag.

On Sunday I even remembered the girls' gifts for a birthday party straight after church. As we were leaving church, our 6-year-old fell and cut her knee. Real blood! And an injured knee with a party looming. Despite the delay, we made it to the party just two minutes late, only to find a note on the door: "We've gone to the Discovery Zone in Redwood City - sorry!" Of course, when I checked the invitation, we were actually 32 minutes late. So we headed home for the address and a street directory. Redwood City is miles away, but better late than never. The end of the party meant Dad would soon be home!

We soon discovered that Dad wasn't nearly home - the minivan had broken down. I'm a member of the emergency road service, but he isn't. So after contacting a mechanic about where to take the car and dispersing the children, I left to meet my husband so we could have the car towed.

This weekend was not exactly typical, but neither was it unique. No-one was killed or injured, nor were there any major traumas. Just the ordinary stuff of life. You can probably recall worse.

What can we say about these days? Firstly, some things in life are beyond our control. Well-maintained cars sometimes break down in inconvenient places. Children fall over and hurt themselves. Every person is marred by sin; children are naturally self-centred and incapable of seeing the larger picture at times (even wonderful children capable of much better!). We must live with these things.

I remember a significant time years ago when my husband was away. I had a 10-week-old baby, and 2-, 3- and 5-year-olds. The hat rail in the hall fell off the wall, the curtain rails in the family room fell down, the shower door come out of its runners and the car broke down. I had to leave my 89-year-old grandmother in the car with the baby while I ran down the freeway in the rain for help. Which of them would protect the other? These things were out of my control.

I've learnt to stop, to take a few seconds to breathe, to think, to talk with God. More importantly, to listen. We only have to live one moment at a time. It's tempting to rehearse the stresses of the past few days and anticipate the next few. That only pushes the pressure over the limit.

However, not all the pressures on 'those days' are out of my control. I think I plan carefully, but I still have lots to learn.

Reflecting quietly on the day is like taking a warm shower after an afternoon digging in the garden. God promises wisdom to those who ask. I need his wisdom to know myself and arrange my time fruitfully. When I neglect to check birthday invitations carefully, I'm too busy. When I book up too much social contact I often feel empty and disconnected when it happens. Then I don't have the poise needed to respond to energetic, verbal children who have their own moods and ups and downs.

So 'those days' need a short-term survival mechanism and a longer term strategy. They'll keep coming with different faces. That's life. But when they do, may our faces more and more show God's grace and glory.

A MODERN MARTYR

A beam of sunlight shoots through an opening in the clouds and transforms the sea before our eyes. There's no colour quite like coastal sea water in afternoon sunlight. Turquoise, my favourite colour.

We're here. It was the usual scurry getting away—even for an overnight trip we need a lot of stuff. Sometimes it's a drag to be the family administrator. My job used to be called homemaking but today it's more administration: organisation, transport, facilitating things happening. Occasionally I feel capable only of making life happen for everyone else in the family. Is there anything left inside to live life myself?

The question haunted me for years. It triggered super-frustration. I don't mind hard work but some days it felt so overwhelmingly menial that I started to see myself as a household servant rather than a person.

For wives and mothers this is a major spiritual challenge. Surely it's a rare woman indeed who hasn't faced it. What do we do with this resentment? The choices we make about resentment produce a psychological stance or posture that gets set. My grandmother used to jokingly warn against pulling faces. "If the wind changes your face will stay that way."

In our inner world the wind changes slowly and before we know it we've taken a stance towards life. Then incoming experience is filtered through that stance. We're stuck.

The posture might be resentful, angry, frustrated or superior. Women are good at taking the high moral ground as a coping strategy. You may have lived with a Martyr (capital M) or been one yourself. It's horrible. Nothing is ever quite right or quite enough to please a Martyr.

I knew a woman who complained about not receiving surprises, but when her husband did manage to surprise her it was never quite right. He shouldn't have left the children with Grandma overnight because Grandma had too much on her plate already. Besides, the timing wasn't good because she had to prepare a lesson for Sunday school.

Gran is overstretched and communicates with her tone and body language that it's a huge task having everyone home for Christmas. When the adult children suggest bringing all the food between them or even holding the function at one of their homes, Gran is upset and hurt that they don't want to come home or think she's unable to cope with it.

Few of us mothers are completely clean when it comes to adopting a martyr posture to cope with our servant role. It's delicious for a moment, but empty and bitter for others to live with.

God shocked me some years ago. He confronted the martyr in me and has been steadily digging it out of my soul since. When I feel a subtle sense of resentment rising up I'm learning to see it for what it is.

My first choice is to quieten down inside and suspend feelings. Acting positively is always better than reacting negatively. I give my feelings a chance to catch up with the positive. They don't have to call the tune. At this precise point faith comes into the picture. Am I resentful that my life is dominated by other people's needs and plans? I expose that to God. No good trying to hide it. Then I do my best to give positively, in faith that God will work it out. Neither his purposes nor mine are served by dishonesty, so I mustn't pretend anything. When the time is right or I'm able to, I share how I feel, but the feelings haven't dominated my behaviour in the meantime.

My husband notices how I am. Living with one who doesn't notice or care is another kettle of fish.

Paradoxically, more transparency and honesty about feelings goes hand in hand with being less dominated by them. Now I try to expose feelings directly. No more withdrawing into manipulation or the martyr position. Somehow struggles can be suspended more easily and I can put feelings aside to receive grace from God to respond positively.

So in spite of the fact that this seaside rendezvous was not my idea, even though all the organisation fell on me, here I am ready for a wonderful 24 hours away! There really is no colour like the turquoise of coastal sea water sparkling in the afternoon sun.

SINGING AT RED LIGHTS

*ave you noticed how often a green traffic light turns red just as you arrive? Then you find yourself sitting unable to move at a completely empty intersection. I remember just this situation. At any other time the Middle East expert on the radio would have sounded eloquent. Right then his voice grated. There were no cars in any direction and I couldn't move a centimetre.

Frustrated at the red light, a sudden insight caused me to gasp inwardly. How like my current position spiritually. For several years I served in children's ministries and focused on my own young children. All the while I was figuring out that women's ministry and evangelism were what I really wanted to do. Then, in a new community and new church, an opportunity to lead women's ministry emerged. Yet in my prayers the Lord consistently said, "I don't give you permission".

Life brings tasks we don't anticipate and God uses experience to teach and shape us for later work. That's obvious and familiar. But exactly what he is doing, or how a current experience relates to what he has done before, often eludes me. When God has pointed in a certain direction but no opportunity opens up to move ahead, that's frustrating. If opportunity stares me in the face and I still can't move ahead that's also very frustrating. Waiting at a red light as cars surge across before my eyes at least makes sense. But it sure feels weird when the intersection is empty. So little time and so much to do.

Time comes up a lot in conversation. Like an overcoat we have to wear but find irritating, time chafes us. No-one can live outside of time, yet we're all uncomfortable living in it.

"Is it only a week since we arrived? It feels like ages ago."

"Can it really be ten years since he left? I can hardly believe it. Seems like yesterday."

Have you noticed how contradictory our perceptions of time can be? Stretching out to unbearable length or contracting to a tiny span, time is very athletic.

Time is just different from God's point of view. Our point of view is changing, too. Einstein and modern physicists have opened new vistas. But the Bible gave us hints all along. In Psalm 90:4 Moses wrote, "For a thousand years in your sight are like a day that has just gone by, or like a watch in the night."

Echoing Moses, many generations later, Peter wrote, "With the Lord a day is like a thousand years and a thousand years are like a day. The Lord is not slow in keeping his promise as some understand slowness" (2 Peter 3:8,9). These passages may not comfort emotionally but we can't ignore them in dealing with the frustration of waiting.

God has stated clearly he is making us like Jesus. "But we know that when he appears we shall be like him, for we shall see him as he is" (1 John 3:2). We read in Ephesians 1:12 that we were chosen so that we, who hope in Christ, might be for the praise of his glory. Our raison d'être is to display God's glory, to be trophies of his grace. He is much more concerned about what he is achieving in us than what we are achieving for him. They are connected of course. But first things must come first. Priority number 1 is enjoying God and displaying what he is like in the situation we are in. Getting to where we think we should be comes lower down the list.

As my van idled at the red light I pictured a vast network of lights controlling traffic flow throughout the city. Those computers aren't perfect. They aren't God. But they serve a great purpose, coordinating life at a higher level than my individual schedule. God is perfect and he, too, co-ordinates life at a much higher level of complexity than my individual path.

I want to wait on him fruitfully. I will breathe gently and decelerate stress when I feel frustration rising. I will turn my inner self towards him and ask to be expanded. Break me out of my narrow focus, Lord. Loosen my fingers from the steering wheel. Let times of waiting loosen me from my focus so I can grasp hold more deeply of yours.

Paul and Silas sang in jail; I might as well sing at red lights.

HELP! I'M SINKING!

lmost in tears, my 12-year-old son sat dejectedly on the sofa. "I have so many problems. Just so many problems."

The problems were various pieces of homework to get in and a crucial lost piece of paper. As a mother my heart went out to him. On one hand it seemed faintly amusing to think of a child with "so many problems". On the other hand it made me sad to hear him saying such unhappy and serious grown-up things about his life.

As usual in that situation I comforted him, trying to speak gently and patiently, even though he didn't want to be comforted. "I know it feels overwhelming. But it will work out. You always get through."

Mumble, mumble. Arms crossed.

"The best thing to do now is go to bed and have a good sleep. We'll pray about the lost paper. You'll be able to work better in the morning."

Hmph.

We did pray about it. He did go to bed and he did get through his crisis.

I find it so helpful being a mother. In retrospect, so many situations my children present and so many of their reactions seem uncomfortably like mine. Responding as the mother gives me a little taste of how God must see me at such times.

Often I feel overwhelmed by the number of things I need to do and remember. Help! I'm sinking!

When I panic my brain function changes from being focused in thinking to being focused in emotion. Panic freezes the head and actually blocks my ability to effectively solve the problems I'm facing. It's a horrible feeling. And one that most of us know. All I can think at such times is "I have so many problems, just so many problems" or thoughts to that effect.

There are times I need to picture God as my Father, my dear, dear Father, saying, "The best thing to do now is go to bed and have a good sleep. I'll help you with all you have to do and you'll function better in the morning."

Of course, it might not be appropriate to go to bed. It might be 10 am. The equivalent or better action is to take some time out to relax and concentrate on God. If you consistently find yourself in panic mode, then you're overstretched and need to revise some basic commitments in your life. However, you can't necessarily do that at the moment of crisis.

How can we escape from panic?

Firstly, stop and calm down. Breathe slowly and stop repeating to yourself all the things you have to do or all the things that are going wrong. It's this repeating over and over of all the problems that causes the panic. While I'm loading layer upon layer of difficulty on my head, I'm digging a deeper and deeper pit for myself. My creativity vapourises. My reasoning grinds to a complete halt and I become incapable of anything but rehearsing my woes.

The rehearsal is verbal or visual or both. Words flashing across the screen of my mind. Pictures whirling around like a spinning top. This must stop.

Slowed breathing helps. Doing something irrelevant to all the pressure can break the cycle and help restore perspective. The (perhaps underrated) practice of list-making forces you into a logical and convergent groove and gets the tasks out of your head and onto something outside you. It also helps break down and quantify the tasks you have to do.

Secondly, remember who God is. Remember your standing with

him. Remind yourself of his plans and perspectives as you know them.

Eliza Doolittle sang in *My Fair Lady*, "Without you twirling it the world still spins, without you pulling it the tide comes in." At moments of panic we need to address such reminders to ourselves. The sun has always risen and set whether I did all I wanted or not. And it always will.

When I remember God's plans and take some time to renew my trust in him - for this moment of need, for this point of pressure, for this list of jobs - then I can go on. And it's amazing how often solutions start to roll. Creative ideas about delegation come. A clearer sense of priorities emerges. Renewed focus and energy surge through the little grey cells. Or I just feel free to leave the list on the table and put myself to bed.

Thank you, Lord, that your plan is not for panic but for peace and productivity. I will wait on you and renew my strength and mount up with wings like an eagle.

BEATEN DOWN

"*I*t's been a hard week. Just the same old stuff I guess," she said calmly as we began our prayer time. I watched her lovely face and listened as she described her week. Her young children had been unsettled, communication with her husband less than scintillating. He was stressed and preoccupied. She was intelligent, articulate, lovely inside and out, and devoted to Jesus. We prayed in her light and pleasant living room with roses blooming outside the window.

"What is the most common feeling women struggle with?" I wondered aloud. My own answer came swiftly and even as the words formed in my mind, her answer matched it exactly. "Worthlessness". Like an epidemic it infects our homes, shopping malls, offices and churches. Watching people gather for worship on Sundays, I see so many faces subdued or strained. We feel beaten down. By what? Life? Our own failure?

When a friend shares feelings of worthlessness it is natural to remind her of the positive qualities we see in her. We want to correct the balance of her perception. My friend with the roses blooming is a careful, creative mother and committed to her marriage in spite of struggles. When she feels she is doing abysmally at life, she needs friends to remind her of the bigger picture.

Friends won't always be there when we need them, though. We

have to learn to speak balance to ourselves. For years now counsellors have been talking about 'self-talk'. We engage in a constant running commentary on ourselves and our lives. Even ancient Greek philosophers knew our experience is shaped less by what happens than by how we choose to respond. We need to take responsibility for the way we perpetuate our pain by what we repeat to ourselves in our heads.

Imagine a little bug in your ear daily telling you you're a failure. Imagine it giving a running commentary on the last time you yelled at the children and the short cuts you take in your marriage and housekeeping. If it's a biblically literate bug it will bring Scripture into it, outlining the way you let the Lord down in your attitudes and in the myriad things you don't do for him. An eloquent bug.

Wouldn't you squash it?

Well, we all have a little bug like that, or something so similar it doesn't matter. For years we have encouraged it by listening. Are you going to keep on listening or begin to challenge the internal monologue? If you struggle with feeling beaten down you need to bring this self-talk out into the light. What weaknesses and failures are you repeatedly rubbing in your own face? What strengths and gifts are you systematically ignoring? Underneath every feeling of worthlessness lies a set of statements that needs exposure. What is the content of your internal talk? Get it out into the open. Talking to someone else helps but we need to move on to doing it ourselves as well. Changing habits is hard. It takes time, but the time is well spent if the bug gets squashed.

Beyond self-talk is the work of Satan. In Revelation 12:10 he is described as accusing us before God day and night. The bug in our ears speaks with Satan's voice as well as our own. The accuser will whittle us away if we let him. Here is the power of the accusations: they are often true! We need more than just balance to see our strength alongside our weakness. We need forgiveness and healing for our real weakness. No wonder we feel failures. We are failures. But that is not all we are. Jesus' blood covers all the failure. We are forgiven. In 2 Corinthians 5:16 Paul wrote that we no longer regard anyone (including ourselves) from a human point of view. Everything is different in light of Christ's death for us. He goes on in verse 17, "if anyone is in Christ he is a new creation. The old has gone, the new has come." God is in the business of retuning our inner ears to the new frequency of his truth. He will build us up as we relinquish the posture of being beaten down. Get rid of the bug. Tune in to God and listen hard.

THE SANDWICH YEARS

Our new neighbours are lovely. They're so friendly. I managed to connect with the mother over a cup of tea recently, though, and she looked so tired. She has two children just started at school and a baby. The baby is cutting her back teeth, so the nights are broken. They'd also been hosting an elderly relative from interstate who had just left. She was exhausted.

She enjoyed having the visitor, but found it tiring at the same time. In the few quiet spots of the day when she could get something done around the kids' routines, he would suggest an activity.

My mind slid off thinking about the competing needs of different generations. I remembered vividly the short years when I still had my grandmother as well as my babies. I felt as if I was going, going all the time with the demands of very young children. Getting us all out somewhere was a significant achievement. Remember that flush of satisfaction, arriving somewhere with a car full of vaguely clean and happy children?

When our destination was my grandmother's house, I always needed to make a big mental shift on arrival. I wanted so much to give her the attention she deserved, to be quiet in spirit and truly go at her pace for a while. We did have many lovely times just visiting at her house, but I usually felt divided. If we went out somewhere it was even harder. Nan had to move very slowly. It took a long time to get in and out of the car. Stretching between an elderly lady and energetic little children—needing to keep the kids safe and occupied without rushing Nan—wasn't easy. Loving seniors just hate their own slowness; they don't want to be a hindrance. The last thing Nan wanted was to hold us up or be a problem in any way. Some days, though, I felt it was just too hard.

Of course, each season passes quickly enough. But this issue of being stretched in opposite directions by the differing needs of young and old is a big issue. Many women in their forties and fifties are sandwiched between children and ageing parents. One of my friends has both parents failing with regular health crises, and four children of her own aged four to 14, one of them severely disabled. Plus her husband has a senior and demanding role at work. I'd say this woman is stretched.

Both elderly frail and young people need practical help and emotional closeness. But it's different for each. A 14-year-old doesn't need her stockings put on or her arm held going down steps. But she does need new school shoes, help with homework and a listening ear at 10 pm. A 90-year-old doesn't need constant transport to school, sport, youth group, and a friend's place. But she might need her shopping done and the footstool put in place when she sits. She might need some quiet uninterrupted time for a cup of tea and a chat.

Many older women don't like to impose their needs on others who are busy with 'important' activities. But if there's no time for relaxed talking, how is connection made? How do you share both your wisdom and your grief at being unable to help and contribute as in the past?

Life requires flexibility. I believe women strive for it and excel at it. When it's our turn to be sandwiched between the pace of the old and of the young, though, it's a bit like doing emotional calisthenics.

In talking about sharing the gospel, Paul wrote of becoming all things to all people (1 Corinthians 9:22). In another way, that's what sandwich-generation women must do, too. Let's not underestimate the value. Time given to others is precious to the Lord. Relationships are the stuff of life. Memories are made of the time spent with my children. Love and faith are communicated by osmosis when we hang out. Parents and grandparents, too, are unspeakably valuable in my life and the lives of my children. God continues to speak into my life through them, both directly and indirectly. Spending time with them is not a burden, it's a joy.

But let's not underestimate the cost, either. It's only common sense to adjust our expectations accordingly. Let's not expect ourselves to be powering on several other fronts while doing the emotional and timetable workout of the sandwich years.

BORED - LOTS TO DO

"*I*'m bored! There's nothing to do!" Don't you hate that sound? In fact, "I'm bored" is a banned phrase in our home.

As a grown-up (at least sometimes I feel like a grown-up!) I don't ever have the problem of nothing to do. My problem is more likely to be busyness and feeling as if it's a drag. I'm bored but I have lots to do. Life is zooming by and my energies are poured into driving, phoning, shopping, tidying up. There's so little left for those great things I was born to do.

I know I was born to pour myself out for others. We all were. But sometimes it just feels like being poured down the drain. And when you're sitting on the plughole, you can't help but ask, "Am I in the right place, or has there been some big mistake here?"

From time to time this question should be asked. Most times the answer will be "No. No big mistake." It's helpful to review the steps that have brought you to where you are. You chose a certain job. You chose to work or to stay at home. You chose a particular man. You have children etc. Much of the daily routine flows directly from these basic choices. If the review leaves you thinking it's time for a change of direction, then you have some praying and work to do.

If, on the other hand, the review reminds you that God is in control and that he has put you where you are, then I have two suggestions.

Firstly, much of what you do is service to others, even if it doesn't feel that way. Think about who benefits from your daily work (and pray for them). Probably your work mostly serves those you love.

Micah wrote, "What does the Lord require of you but to love mercy and to do justice and to walk humbly before your God?" And Paul wrote, "Whatever you do, do as for the Lord."

God delights in us simply doing what is right—what is in front of our noses—and doing it for his glory. This applies to washing socks and dishes, wiping noses and bottoms, and keeping budgets as much as to anything else. I find it helps me a lot to think of each person as I fold his or her clothes. I imagine the little toes that go into those socks and the little bottoms that go in the pants. I remember how much I love each precious person and remind myself that no-one else in the world has the privilege of such intimacy with my husband and children.

And it is a service of love to do my work well. It makes a difference. Once when I felt very tired of mundane chores, I decided to let the washing go for just two days. On the third morning a couple of children couldn't find clean underwear. Their frustration gushed out. We were late for school and everyone started the day hurried and grumpy.

It was a good experiment in a backwards way. Whenever I get sick of washing I remember that morning and tell myself I am actively creating smooth starts to the day by having lunches cut and washing done. I'm not running a house. I'm creating a home. Each boring component of that is a gift of service and love to my family and to my God. In my head I wrap these tasks in pink paper and lift them up to God with holy hands.

As well as remembering the importance of unimportant work, there is a second suggestion for you if you're in the right place but sitting on the plughole ready for dispatch: Have fun!

A big trap for down-in-the-mouth women is not bothering to make the effort to have fun. Sure, it takes effort. But usually it's worth it. This week, plan something completely different. Go to a movie in the middle of the day. Take a Bible or a sketchbook or nothing to a beautiful garden. Ask a friend to have the children so you can browse in a favourite store or have coffee out. Find a cheap or free concert or recital in the city at lunchtime. Write a poem. Sort old photos and write a few lines about them to include in your album for posterity. Pack a picnic lunch in a basket with a check cloth (preferably blue or red with white). Remember to include a special drink - not just the usual juice. Paint a picture. Arrange time with a friend if you're madly working all the time, or time alone if you're peopled out.

If you are feeling seriously bored with lots to do, then fun is a priority for you this week. And while you're taking time out, remember that giving of yourself to others is valuable. God's point of view is different from ours. He will come to you and be close to you in your rest. Ask him.

He will affirm to you whether you're in the right place. If you are, then don't let the mundane in life overwhelm you. Value your service to others. Have fun. Get off the plughole before the next deluge washes you away, and live!

CHOOSING A BETTER WAY

DIVE INTO THE JOYS

*J*ust a few years ago my life was a blur of babies and pre-schoolers. Half the time I scarcely knew if it was night or day in the endless round of broken sleep, nappy buckets, eating and wiping up. It was a wonderful time and an exhausting time.

So often older parents would say, "Enjoy these years. It gets harder later. These are the golden years." I said nothing, but my parched eyeballs would sink further into their sockets and I'd think, "You've just forgotten."

They must have forgotten the haze of sleep deprivation and the inescapable round of being on call 24 by 7.

I would gaze longingly at families with big kids who brushed their own teeth, went to the toilet by themselves, and walked to the car, climbed in and did up their own seatbelts when it was time to go somewhere. How could those older women call my season "the golden years"? They could sleep through the night. Their kids went to school all day. Obviously they had just forgotten.

Today we had some neighbours in for coffee. A family has moved into the new house next door with two young children and a baby. Another neighbour, with two upper primary children and a high-powered career was lamenting how quickly children grow up.

"Enjoy every minute. I wish I'd spent more time just enjoying my children when they were younger", was her comment to the baby's mother. I agreed. Those days that seemed endless at the time have melted away like a morning mist.

These days, my life is full of decisions and driving, cooking and shopping. My time revolves around four teenagers, all of whom have busy schedules and none of whom yet drive. Where I once spent the day running around in circles, I now spend it driving around in circles. It's a new season.

Plenty of parents bemoan these years. It's emotionally exhausting when you're constantly adapting to changes, being challenged by the children at every turn, making decisions. Schedules and rhythms that made the family cohesive in the past, take a lot more effort to sustain. Individual lives are blossoming and moving in different directions. Sleep may not be broken, but it's still not plentiful. Mum and Dad have to serve and give, but don't seem to be heeded much. I understand those older mothers much better now.

However, our kids are so exciting. Although I'm solid, boring and middle-aged, I understand youth lingo and I'm connected into the vibrant world of the young. I think of my mother-in-law, and her wistful reminiscences of her children living at home. Even though it's 30 years since she was the busy mother of three youth, she still misses the intimacy of that life. She helps me to savour the joys of my current life in spite of its frustrations. In another blink of an eye, I will be an older middle-aged woman with grown independent children. Then I will never experience the daily involvement in my children's lives that is so precious now.

Of course, then I will be able to keep my house more attractive and actually pursue involvements of my own. I should be able to go to bed if I'm tired and not get a call asking to be picked up in the middle of the night.

So what's the conclusion? Every season has its special joys and its costly demands. We have a choice. We can focus on the costs, or on the joys. We can experience every season as the best years of our lives if we will. "To everything there is a season and a time for every purpose under heaven." There's a time for pudgy bottoms and endless cuddles. There's a time for shaping characters and helping to develop skills. There's a time for building adult friendships with children who are becoming adults. There's a time for sleep. There's a time for uninterrupted thought. And there's a time to let go of such luxuries. God reveals himself to us in different ways in different seasons. The more fully we abandon ourselves to the limitations and the joys of each season, the more fully we can know him in all his richness.

So if you want to live your life instead of watching it slip by, take your eyes off the costs of the season you're in. Dive into the joys instead.

I CAN'T STAND IT

❦

*S*ome days it feels as if all my buttons get pushed. How come people know how to do that, especially children?

There used to be a particular male head nurse at work who was very adept at pressing my buttons. Then it was a small group leader at church. Now most often it's the children. I'm not talking about major stress events or overload here, But sometimes the accumulation of little irritations is just too much.

If every part of me feels fine but there's a stone in my shoe, all the beauty of the world around is lost on me. Massed white clouds drifting across a clear blue sky and agapanthus erupting on the footpaths make no impact. My marriage can be great and my life functioning pretty well, but with a stone irritating me it's hard to keep focused on what's going well.

Generally there are particular-shaped stones that are most likely to irritate me and particular parts of me that are sensitive to irritation. The sensitive spots are the areas where I feel weak or self-conscious.

One of my buttons is labelled "Today's not worth living. We never have any fun!" If only my children could see how incredibly well-off they are. Unlike many who are neglected or battered or starving, they are loved, cared for, educated etc. For some reason it doesn't help to point these contrasts out(!).

The last time this button was pushed I felt worn down and conscious that I'm not much fun. It takes most of my energy to keep the family afloat and functional. Spontaneity, creativity and fun are definitely not my long suit. Consequently the "we never have fun" line hit a sensitive spot.

It worries me that our children need ever-increasing levels of fun and stimulation. Are we raising them to be indulged, materialistic little addicts of pleasure? So I didn't take it lying down. But my efforts to hammer home the importance of making fun out of everyday things upset my son (surprise, surprise!). I was cross. He was upset. But we kept talking. I got over being cross and he pushed through being upset. We finally arrived together at the conclusion that he was frustrated about a lack of social contact with his friends.

He learnt it would be better to say, "I have less social life than the other kids and I want to see my friends more". I learnt that my sensitivities about not being much fun caused me to see an attack where I didn't need to. I now realise it's one of the buttons that I need to watch.

Another of my buttons is bad habits. I find it most irritating when children bite nails, or sniff and snort instead of using a handkerchief. Although such things are unpleasant, my child's weakness also sets off inner embarrassment about my own habits. Now I'm in my 40s I should be past them!

One reliable button is "It's not fair. Look what she did to me!" How come children can't see how self-centred they are? When they constantly bicker or clash wills, the irritation is two-fold: it's plain boring and inconvenient to spend time on arbitrating disputes, but worse, there's also a nagging feeling underneath that if I handled them better it wouldn't happen. What's the matter with my parenting? Why do my children behave like this? Maybe they are just feeding back my grumpy voice. Maybe I don't give them enough effective attention. Maybe, maybe ...

No doubt there's some truth in these maybes. If so, I need to deal with it. More sleep can help cut out my grumpy voice. I could ask God to help me keep phone calls and other occupations until children aren't around.

To get a stone out of my shoe I take it off and tip it up. To get a stone out of my insides I need to do the same. I must find the worry or underlying sense of failure. Sometimes it takes prayerful reflection. Sometimes it takes communication and pushing through a conflict. God's desire is to release the power of the Spirit to disconnect our buttons. He cares about everyone and is constantly at work to refine and propel us towards the image of Jesus.

THE POWER OF THANKYOU

*E*ven though it is mid-winter here, yesterday the sky was blue. Magnolias adorned the bare pale grey branches in deep pink and white. Spring smells floated about deliciously. Such a tantalising promise of the earth's renewal again.

Today the sky is grey again and fog obscured the neighbours' houses this morning. Although our winters are mild, grey skies do dampen the spirits. A lovely release of joy in living and gratefulness to God came from such a simple gift as a blue sky.

What was I grateful for? God's incredible, pulsing reality - he is! For God's love for me and all his creation, for a husband who values and loves me, for healthy beautiful children, for food and a warm bed, for ways of serving the body of the church, for trees and magnolias and the smell of spice cake in the oven, for the sense of being a rich woman standing in my place in the tide of humanity, for the certainty that Jesus is coming back. All these things are gifts to me each day. A blue sky in mid-winter simply helps me feel them more vividly.

Once I start thanking God it's amazing how easily more things come to mind. A flow of gratefulness is so near the surface but so easily ignored. If you begin expressing thanks to God, notice what happens in your body as well as your mind. Firstly, you will probably take a deeper breath than normal and your breathing will slow down. An involuntary smile might flicker across your lips and eyes. Next your shoulders may drop a little and your stomach muscles relax and go squishy. A sigh, a slump, another smile.

This is a classic relaxation response in psychological terms. It is the opposite of the stress response. Gratefulness brings a drop in adrenaline. To relax your body, even briefly, is to restore strength and balance and to create emotional space for your priorities to resettle. Tension propels you forward. Rest allows regrouping, focus and renewal. Gratefulness opens the gate into inner rest. We must discipline ourselves to open that gate; it's not our natural bent. Frustration, resentment and disappointment spring much more readily to mind.

Pollyanna's 'glad game' has become a byword for naive gooey unreality. But if you know the God who is there, what a basis you have for great expectations! And for gratefulness. My life contains many unanswered questions and many unfulfilled expectations. Surely every life does. But I know God. He has made me his own, given me eternal work to do and promised to come and take me home.

It sounds trite to say I need to focus on what he has done, who he is and what my hope is. But this is the simple, vital truth. Every day a choice lies before me: to focus on the disappointments and frustrations and gradually sink beneath the tension, or to focus on all I'm sure of and all I have. Isaiah 40:31 says that those who hope in the Lord will renew their strength. They will soar on wings like eagles. Will I trudge today or soar?

Isaiah expresses the tension we live in. We hope in the Lord - for what? Not for what we already see, or else we need not hope. So there is an implicit dissatisfaction with the present. But we are to wait and rest and be renewed. Some versions use "wait on" rather than "hope in". We rest and wait with confidence because we know who the Lord is.

Similar acknowledgment of this tension we live in occurs in Philippians 4:6. Such a familiar verse about thankfulness and so much wisdom for living! "Do not be anxious about anything, but in everything by prayer and petition with thanksgiving, present your requests to God." Presumably there is cause for anxiety. There must be dissatisfaction with the present, or else why would there be petitions and requests?

So why do we present requests with thanksgiving? Because in thanking God we acknowledge who he is. We honour him and show him our awareness of who he is. Secondly, we release tension in ourselves. We create emotional space to remind ourselves of all we are and have; to throw ourselves onto the God we know as Father and redeemer. God knows we need this discipline if we are to know joy, even to survive. So Paul gave the Philippians an instruction, not a suggestion.

"Hope in the Lord!" scripture says, and you will soar like an eagle. "Be thankful!" scripture says, and you will be able to express your desires to God. My prayer is that God will strengthen gratefulness in me. Thank you, Lord!

FAMILIES THAT PLAY TOGETHER...

❦

"*L*et's go straight to the beach!" the children yelled almost in unison. We'd hardly set eyes on the sparkling sea or whiffed the seaweed, but it felt like summer holidays for the children.

For all our married life we've made this trek to the same beach in January. Our tent has served us well. The caravan park has improved a little: the showers and toilet block had a facelift and I enjoy the patches of lawn and bright flowers among the dust and dirt of the park.

Nevertheless, I have to confess it's been an effort. Four babies crawling and toddling in the dirt wasn't really fun. Washing nappies with a trough and wringer felt silly with an automatic machine idle at home. Settling children for sleep wasn't easy with only canvas between us and noisy neighbours. But mostly it was the dirt that got me down.

What about the attractions? Well, I love being with extended family, who camp with us. We laugh a lot and talk a lot, drink coffee and play games. I don't know how many families do that but it's precious.

In the years of little children adult time was scarce. It required staying up late—costly when the day starts at 6 am. When by 10 am you've already changed nappies and clothes, produced breakfast, been to the playground and the beach with the stroller and used up all your bright ideas for keeping children quiet and happy, the day sure feels long.

I used to think of those weeks as a change but hardly a holiday. However, our commitment to this annual experience has connected us to a long family tradition, wider and deeper than it seems. Our children are the fourth generation of the family to holiday here. The gathering is now around 25 strong. The children fish and snorkel not only with Dad but also with uncles and cousins. Now they beat us at Take Two and Scrabble and stay up late to play Monopoly. One grown-up nephew brought his girlfriend this year; while they had a special breakfast with Nanna and Grandad, our children had cereal and toast with an auntie and uncle.

Middle-aged brothers teach the clan of children to clean fish and squid. Then they barbecue it to perfection. I love to watch young faces smiling at the older generation's banter. Family ribbing follows much the same pattern each year but always seems delightful.

We all have our place in the system. Grandad teaches snorkelling. He taught me 24 years ago when I was engaged, just entering the family. Nanna is the hostess extraordinaire—any missing children can probably be found drinking raspberry cordial and eating cream biscuits in her caravan. Our adult cousins offer the children milk Milo when they play board games together. Milk Milo is strictly rationed at home.

This year Uncle Ray had heart surgery and Uncle Chris started a new job. One cousin married and brought her husband from inter-state to join us. Various children started or finished high school. Three nephews acquired girlfriends and brought them all. What a rich, rich tapestry a family's life is, especially when the love of God intertwines it. And the pattern comes together uniquely on our summer holiday.

It has become an institution. As thoughtful Christian parents, Nanna and Grandad braved the dirt and flies to give their children a holiday. They little realised what they were starting. Now all of us, in our turn, do the same. Along with our normal comforts, we leave behind TV, phone, calendar and Nintendo 64. We digest each year's experience over cards and supper and move forward as a family. There have been challenges and occasionally conflict to resolve over the years, but with God's grace we've all emerged stronger.

I would never have had the energy to create all this—it came with my wedding ring. Although I still have my moments when we're packing, I wouldn't swap the tradition for anything. As the children roll into bed each night exhausted but happy, I know the effort's worth it. God's here with us—at the heart of it, just as he's at the heart of family.

With the years of little children behind I can sit back and be grateful. Flushed with the virtuous satisfaction of building family memories, I might even be motivated to go for a snorkel.

THE ART OF LISTENING

*Y*ears ago a friend in church surprised me. Her son often played at our house with my son, although neither of them had much attention from me. There were generally lots of people in the house and other children to attend to. On this occasion, my friend laughingly described her son telling her off for not listening. "When I'm at Merilyn's, she stops and looks at my eyes when I talk. You don't."

I was astonished. "It's not true", I protested. "Just ask my kids!" Fortunately our friendship was resilient, and interestingly enough, that friend is now a counsellor.

Listening sounds so simple, but in the complexity of life it proves elusive. It's a beautiful thing to be heard. Peacefully, openly listening to another has great power. It defuses anger and frustration, relieves tension and stress, connects people's hearts, minds and spirits, and oils the wheels of social life. It even streamlines decision making.

Many of us women are gifted at listening. Many have been involved in pastoral care in churches or Bible study groups, and we've been convinced of the importance of listening. Although we sometimes feel inadequate and powerless to help, we have seen that other women really appreciate being able to share.

How about on the home front, though? There's an old saying,

"Cobblers' wives go barefoot and doctors' wives die young." I wonder about that for caring, listening people, too. Do we remember to listen to others when we're out, but get caught in routine busyness at home?

Listening to someone requires being quiet inside. If my mind is busy I can't concentrate on what you are saying. It takes effort to quieten my mind. It's a discipline.

For women, home is a workplace, so there's plenty for our minds to be busy about with the practical demands of every day. The job of mothering adds more complexity. Because we're so eager to protect and teach and train our children, we're constantly processing what they say with a view to giving instruction.

Consequently, in the place where we most want to be caring we're vulnerable to failure. It's perhaps hardest to quieten our minds and make space to properly listen when we're with our families.

I am regularly brought up short about this. It's embarrassing how many times in a week one of my teenagers exclaims in exasperation, "Just listen, will you?"

Of course there's more to communication than listening. We do have a responsibility to train our children. However, a basic, foundational building block of relationship is listening. How can we know how our husbands, children or housemates are feeling if we don't listen and take time to reflect on what we hear? Sometimes I need to suspend my perspective, my hopes and fears, anxieties and frustrations about someone in my family. I need to spend a little time hearing them and thinking about their perspective, hopes and fears, anxieties and frustrations. It can be quite weird getting a glimpse of myself through someone else's eyes.

We all know this, but sometimes need reminding to do it. How about this week making a priority of listening to your family? Take little windows of opportunity to receive, without assessment, some news or views of your children. Quality listening doesn't fit into real life in great slabs. It's the little windows of opportunity we must look for. How about sitting down for five minutes with a child when they have their afternoon snack? How about spending ten (or 30) minutes over a cup of coffee with your husband and giving your attention to him? If you did that every day, face to face, it could change your marriage. Eye-to-eye quiet listening time is more precious than gold.

God, who always listens and always wants to be listened to, will be right there with you.

WHO FIRST?

*R*egular exercise is a great idea. I've been working on establishing the habit for quite a while. Several days a week I plod around the corner to the local gym to push, pull, huff and puff. Staffed exclusively by men but frequented by women, the gym brings in a female trainer for women wanting individual attention.

And what a woman! She epitomises the benefits of regular exercise. Not an ounce of fat on her beautifully developed, finely-tuned torso. Her shoulders look as strong as most men's. Her thighs and calves could deliver a formidable kick. I haven't engaged her services myself. She exudes a kind of confidence and self-absorption that I don't warm to.

Last week, while I grappled with an upper-body machine, she worked with another woman on a machine nearby. The customer was slim and attractive, perhaps in her late twenties. They were discussing her potential for a truly excellent 'rear-end'. The body part in question looked excellent to me already.

I couldn't help but hear the conversation.

Customer: "Nick isn't a morning person. He goes back to sleep after the alarm and then expects me to wake him up. He seems to think it's my responsibility to get him to work on time in the mornings. I'm too busy in the mornings. I have to get ready myself."

Trainer: "That's right. Remember what we've talked about. It's really important what you put into your body. You have to eat right in the morning."

Customer: "Yeah, I know. Nick doesn't get that. He's quite selfish in the morning. He's a great person—don't get me wrong—just not a morning person."

Trainer, pointing finger: "You come first. You are number one. You have to look after yourself or else you start eating rubbish and neglecting your exercise and it all falls apart. You're number one, and he's number two. Even when you have that baby, you're number one, the baby's number two and he's number three. That's the way it is."

My mind was buzzing. I wondered if the trainer had any children. I thought about the shock that customer was in for when she took her first baby home from hospital. When she was several months sleep-deprived and yanked from slumber by a crying baby at 2 am, should she roll over, replace her earplugs and snooze off again? After all, if her body didn't keep functioning it would "all start falling apart".

Casting my mind back, I tried to imagine living out the trainer's words. With a grumpy, tired two-year-old and a baby with a dirty nappy and a husband tired from an extra heavy patch at work plus a big presentation looming, what would it have meant to put myself first? The pressing necessities of life mixed with that priority would have been a guaranteed recipe for frustration. Left to simmer a while, there would have soon been a bubbling pot of resentment.

I can't see the "You are number one" formula being nearly robust enough to get a woman through real life.

By contrast, the Sunday school formula is JOY—Jesus first, Others second and Yourself last. This is not politically correct, but it is more promising than the gym lady's plan. The trouble is, it seems to have produced a lot of women out of touch with their inner selves, stiff and indirect in their communication. If it's selfish to express feelings and desires, then doing so becomes taboo, and you have to resort (subconsciously) to manipulative behaviour and communication.

The "Jesus first" part is right. Jesus told us to love God with everything in us. The other part of his instruction was to love our neighbours as ourselves. What a revelation the first time I heard someone say that we had better love ourselves, or how would our neighbours get on? In real life, sometimes it's more important to attend to someone else's need first and sometimes more important to attend to our own.

Why do we set ourselves up in separation from those we love and serve? Let's truly accept ourselves as persons needing attention and love in the system rather than pretending we have no needs. Then, consulting Jesus first, let's use our creative energies to see that we all get cared for as well as possible.

Now that the children are all at school, I can think about myself more. Free to huff and puff at the gym!

SLAVE OR FREE?

"I don't know why I feel so tired and grumpy. I just do." My friend brushed her hair from her eyes and sighed. "The weekend away was more restful than I expected and nothing bad had happened at home. The kids just hadn't done what they were supposed to." The rest of us, gathering for a prayer meeting, all nodded as one. We are all parents of a number of teenagers.

"I'm getting to feel like the unpaid servant around the house." More nods around the circle. "Looking beyond yourself to what's happening in the lives of people around you is just basic Christian living, isn't it? I confront and raise the issues, but I feel like I'm becoming a nagging mother. I don't want to be a nagging mother."

This struck a chord. We tossed around a few ideas. Each of us had apparently toyed with the possibility of just stopping work for a week. What would happen if we did no washing or ironing, cooking or tidying for a week? Those who had tried this approach had only tried it on a limited basis. They had not touched a particular room or some such. That didn't work. It didn't take long for the mess to be unbearable to the mother.

All parents know the guidelines and expectations have to be clear. There have to be consequences but it's hard to follow through. Open defiance, hostility or deceitfulness have to be singled out for quick and focused attention. However, the tedium of daily little chores feels much harder to get a grip on.

If a family member doesn't take out the rubbish, or set the table, or pack away homework clutter when asked, the whole family system just gets clogged and cumbersome. Bells don't ring to say these matters are serious parenting stuff. It just feels like boring, tedious hard work.

A number of times I have retreated into the frustrated martyr position.

"Would you please bring me your dirty clothes and your lunchbox."

"Do I have to right now? I'm busy."

"I would appreciate it now. I want to get a load of washing on."

"Why does it matter so much if it's now?"

"Oh look, forget it. I can't be bothered with this. Just forget all about it."

I always know immediately this is wrong. It's wounding. I regret it.

Often it's easier and more peaceful to do it yourself. However, that doesn't work as a long-term strategy either. You wear out and feel like a failure at training children for real life.

Mothers who go out to work seem to have a better handle on this one. The whole family has to pull up its socks to make the system work. However, I don't intend to complicate my life with a job to force my children to pull their weight more. Perhaps a little taste … next year I have two commitments that will take me away for a couple of weeks. I will give some basic instructions in cooking, washing and layout of the kitchen cupboards leading up to these big events and then we'll see what happens.

Sometimes you have to leave the system to provoke a change.

I wish I could say I always set clear consequences for failure to do tedious chores and then follow through. However, I can't. I aim for consistent reminders and consequences when I can manage them. Sometimes the situation is too complicated or I'm just too tired.

In real life I occasionally do it all myself. Peace. And sometimes I give myself time off in a limited way. Last night I felt a bit crazy.

The busyness and pressure of the end-of-year schedule had been constant and something in me said "Enough".

We had a scratch tea—everyone in together getting eggs and leftovers, being zany together. We played cards and cracked corny jokes and talked in stupid voices. Everyone was as helpful and cooperative as they could be. It did me the world of good.

Then next year there's the prospect of a longer spell off duty from keeping kids focused. They are old enough. They will have to pull together to manage.

My prayer is often for poise, to respond not react; for sleep so that there's a chance to be poised; for consistency to stick at the task of training and for opportunities to change the system by stepping out of it. Lord, save me from being a nagging mother. Make me a free woman who serves, not a slave.

A GENTLE ANSWER

*H*ave you ever noticed you can't make anyone feel sorry? All the talking and explaining in the world can't reach into someone's heart and force them to feel anything.

It seems silly, or at least ironic, to insist on an apology from a child who has been out of line. "I'm not sorry. So you want me to lie, do you?" my children have asked many times.

The response is always the same: "No, I can't make you feel sorry and I don't want you to say it if it's not true. You do have to apologise, though. I insist on that."

"I apologise", through clenched jaw.

As a parent, I can only legislate behaviour, not feelings. I insist on the outward form of acknowledging wrong and can only pray for the inward experience to come.

Any day of parenting requires a string of decisions and rulings. "Do I have to sweep the floor today?" "Can I skip flossing my teeth tonight?" "Can I have a friend over after school?" "He really hurt me!" "But he hurt me first." "I'm going to play Nintendo 64 now. OK?" "Don't you think it's fair for me to sit in the front on the way to school? She always gets to sit in the front." "They leave me out." "No-one listens to me. He interrupts all the time and you don't do anything about it." "It's so late. Do I have to do music practice?" "Tell him to stop singing. It drives me crazy and he knows it."

One night recently one of our children asked to do music practice in the kitchen/living area. Getting practice routines established again after holidays is quite an effort and the practice is often later than ideal. It's tempting to bend over backwards to help. I knew, however, the volume of the instrument would block out any other conversation or phone calls in that part of the house. Although no other family members were present at that moment, I couldn't face the noise or the arguments if others did come in wanting to talk to me. I said no.

This was not an acceptable response. "But why not? There's no reason. No-one else is here."

"I said no. Music practice should be in your room."

"But ..."

"Enough! I'm not saying it again! Go and do your practice. Do what you've been asked to do without any more arguments."

That is probably one of the hardest requirements in the world. "Do it without more arguments". She flounced off, clearly hurt and angry.

I sighed. I have been wearied and perplexed for some time by the hardness and inflexibility of this child. How can the young be so determined and unbending? She perceives life in black-and-white terms right now. Black is black, white is white, others are wrong and she is right.

It's hard work fighting for your place in a family of four children. Even some grown-ups never seem to stop that fight. They will justify themselves in conflict situations as relationships crash and burn around them. The hardest thing in the world is to give in.

Well, I repented of my harsh tone while she was playing away in her room. The decision was right, I was confident of that. But the tone was hard. I had been already steeling myself for the emotional fallout to follow. As I finished cleaning up the kitchen, I realised how I've been standing my ground and justifying myself in conflicts with her lately. I was becoming as bad as her at justifying myself.

After the music practice finished (I didn't want to interrupt), I went into her room and apologised for speaking so harshly. She wrapped her arms around me and said she was sorry too. We had a big hug.

What a joy! And what a surprise! It wasn't what I expected at that moment.

All the following week I remembered that hug. How close I'd been to hammering home her inappropriate behaviour rather than acknowledging my own. We would have missed something special.

In Proverbs it says, "A soft answer turns away wrath." I've been savouring the sweetness and truth of that lately. I'm asking God for grace in weariness to stand my ground but give a soft answer.

HOPING AGAINST HOPE

"I never gave up praying that Dad would soften." Deep feeling flowed through the speaker's voice. "One of my fondest hopes was that he would recognise his need of Jesus. And my heart yearned to be with him when he died."

"He did find God too. It was wonderful, but I wasn't with him when he died." He told us he'd been teaching overseas when his father died. Every precaution had been taken to avoid them being apart. Doctors had indicated there was time to spare, etc etc.

Why would God grant the larger request and not the smaller, seemingly easier one? It was disappointing. It hurt. Yet, even as the tears slid down his cheeks, his confidence in God's kindness shone.

My mind wandered to my own family experience. For years I had prayed for my father's conversion. I had pictured Dad as a Christian and savoured the prospect of his influence inside and outside our family. I had suggestions about the kind of man who could reach Dad with the gospel, even a particular person who fitted the bill. Strangely, God didn't heed my suggestions.

Eventually, Dad did become a Christian. He slipped into the kingdom on the last day that he was capable of thinking straight before sliding into death. No opportunities to influence others, no big 'impact for the gospel'. I had pictured great things early in my dealings with God about Dad. Great things based on scripture, or at least on my understanding of it. Were my pictures full of faith and promise fulfilled? No. Did God hear my prayers? Yes.

Imagination is a great gift. We read about God using everything for good and images start flowing. It's easy to picture our church's youth program making a radical difference in the neighborhood, or the Bible study group powerfully impacting lives. We can redesign people close to us in a moment. Imagination colours life and inspires prayer.

On the other hand, life brings painful disappointments. Many people I love do not know Jesus, in spite of prayer and in spite of God's power to make himself known. I have seen that power and how ruthlessly he can pursue someone in love, and yet ...

A couple of years ago, I was so excited to share the gospel with friends who were interested in a Bible study group. We studied Mark's gospel and talked directly about Jesus' claims about himself. In a world where few people seem interested to talk about Jesus, they were. But they didn't get to know him. We are good friends. I know they like and respect me, and yet ...

Imagined applications of God's promises fuel our prayers, which is great, and yet are so often our desires are not borne out in reality. Hopes get dashed. Some of us have given up hoping because disappointment hurts so much. So we have to ask, "What are we hoping for?"

God is making us like Jesus. 1 John 3:1-3 says we will be like him when we see him. In Colossians 3:1-4 Paul speaks of our life being hidden with Christ in God. When he appears we also will appear with him in glory. I call that an exciting prospect. More broadly, we know that Christ will be called Lord by every living being. Ephesians 1 and Philippians 2 make that clear. There will be no more pain and no more tears according to Revelation 21:1-4. We are inheritors of incredible hope that God is working in his world and will finish what he has started.

Growing into our inheritance is the challenge. While imagination is a powerful tool in meditation and prayer, it has also "participated in the Fall", as Richard Foster points out in his book, *Celebration of Discipline*. "Imagination helps to anchor our thoughts and center our attention", Foster goes on. Imagination helps us grow into God's vision. The problem is our pictures of God's plan aren't always right, even when they're good pictures. Disappointments are major chances to refine and re-align. By keeping our faces resolutely towards God in his goodness, we give him the chance to use our hurts. He will wean us off escapist fantasy and ground our imagination and our hopes in his reality. We have to let him.

PARENTING ISN'T A SPECTATOR SPORT

*I*sn't there an old saying, "The longest way round is the shortest way home"? There's a lot of truth in that when it comes to parenting.

Last night our youngest child turned up her nose at her weekly allowance. If she had lost that many ticks on her chart and only got that much allowance, it wasn't worth having. She turned her back on the miserable pile of coins and disappeared in a huff. The requirements on the weekly chart are basic, at least from our point of view. Keeping her bedroom tidy, being ready for school on time, music practice and a simple daily chore. We even allow days off. Yet the emotional effort required from me to maintain these charts is considerable. Perhaps maintaining consistent expectations is the point; not yielding to the tug to bend in the children's direction.

Training children takes effort. It's so much easier to woo them. It isn't difficult for me to tidy up the dirty clothes and pack away the doll equipment from a weekend play session with a friend. After all, it isn't like the chaos of toddlers. So sometimes I can't be bothered instructing one more time or checking to see if it's done one more time. It is easier simply to do the job and move on.

After taking the line of least resistance for a while though, there comes a crunch. Soon you feel ignored. A sense of being ineffective starts to weigh you down. A friend's daughter stayed overnight this week, and I couldn't help noticing how organised she was. She hovered around me as I packed six lunches, wanting to help. At home she gets her own—and makes coffee for her dad. I wonder how many other mothers pack all the lunches each morning?

Parenting older children requires a different kind of effort. One of the textbook characteristics of adolescence is being argumentative. I always smile when I read that—how much research did it take to discover the obvious? The persistence of our teenagers can be a marvel to behold. Our oldest child needs lots of debate. He is struggling to adapt to a major change in his life, and we regularly come in for criticism over it. After several extended discussions between him and me, there seemed nowhere to go.

Next time the subject arose, I referred him to his dad. So one night the household was treated to an energetic discussion (to put it mildly) between the two of them. It was hard to concentrate on anything else, the conversation was so interesting. Points were raised and developed on each side. Maybe nothing startlingly new came up, but they heard each other. Dad offered solutions I hadn't suggested, which our son considered before rejecting them.

It would have been easier to cut the talk. "We've gone over and over this—we're not discussing it any more." Often that is the best response, but not on this occasion. The investment of time and energy appears justified: spirits are more robust in the family since, and we are praying more specifically about his needs. The line of least resistance would have sown seeds of greater dissatisfaction and distance between us.

In the case of the disenchanted daughter, I injected a tiny bit of wooing with extra kisses in bed. However, I also used a firm, positive approach with, "Darling, this week you won't lose so many ticks on the chart and get such a small allowance, because you are going to do so much better. I will help you a bit this morning, and then you can do it!" We'll see how the week develops. I'm going to resist taking the easy way when the pressure is on.

Parenting is a long-term job. We won't get to see all the results in this life, but in Proverbs we are told that, if we train children in the way they should go, they will not depart from it in their old age. What feels easier isn't necessarily best or easier on us in the long term. In fact, the longest way around often is the shortest way home. So some privileges must go until the performance on the charts is higher, and I must maintain our expectations with firm cheerfulness instead of bending.

I think I will keep packing the lunches though.

RACKED WITH INDECISION

ow do you know you're in love?" I remember asking married friends in my late teens. "How do I know if he's the one I should marry?"

"You'll just know." Oh, that frustrating reply!

The man in question wasn't the one I married. Now, more than 20 years later, I can see that the need to ask the question was itself the answer. When my husband came along, I didn't ask anyone. I just knew.

But how do we know these things? Of course, the answer must include the Holy Spirit. Praise God he's there. But many decisions are still not automatically clear. Most of us have times of agonising indecision.

Should we take the promotion my husband has been offered? Is it a natural time to leave the church or would we be leaving things unfinished? How about the children? Would they be able to cope with moving schools? So many questions whiz around and around the central point: Is this what God wants me to do?

James wrote, "If any of you lacks wisdom, you should ask God, who gives generously to all without finding fault, and it will be given to you" (James 1:5). There's a clear instruction and promise. When the need for a decision arises, the first step is to ask God, with confidence in his generosity.

In my experience, though, that's just a first step. Waves of contrary feelings usually follow. One day I'll be caught up with all the possibilities of option A. The next day the pitfalls and hassles come much more clearly into focus and my fancy skips off along the highways and byways of option B.

In this past month I've been faced with an unexpected decision. My decade at home with pre-school children served to clarify a desire to work with women in the church. With our youngest child entering her second year of school, I had just started praying and talking with our pastor's wife about working together to develop work amongst women in our church.

Then, cutting straight across that, came a request to stand as co-president of the Parent and Teachers Association (PTA) at our children's school. This was not what I was looking for. Upsetting events in the school community over the past year had produced a particular need in the PTA and a teacher approached me with an earnest request for my involvement.

I couldn't reject it out of hand, so I asked God for clear confirmation: via approaches from others and in verification from my husband.

Two weeks of tossing and turning at night and waking early followed. Excitement about the possibilities of being God's channel in the school alternated with longings to see the women in our church released and built up.

One day I would find that school entanglements felt jaded, stuffy and irrelevant. But the next, a sense of God's pleasure in having his own as a channel in the school would warm my bones. Around and around.

There were several key elements in the process for me. The first was discussing it with a few friends and then handing their views to God. The second was to take seriously my feelings. In making decisions I don't ignore feelings. I feel the grief of losing the opportunity opening up in the church. I feel the sadness of missing out on God's action in relationships at school. Then I hand the feelings to God.

Finally, I face the intrusion of my pride into the situation. In this case, it was flattering to be sought out over a delicate situation at the school. Pride always has a part in everything. For me it's important to acknowledge and articulate the pride in each situation, to my husband at least. Then the pitfalls awaiting me because of my pride usually become clear in my mind. I ask God to protect me.

Through this cycle of expression, facing what's in me, yielding it to God and waiting, my spinning self finally comes to rest. And to decision, and confidence about what God wants.

Previous expectations, various feelings, a range of fears about missing out, all look like clear spokes of a wheel. The hub of the wheel is a sense of the Holy Spirit's quiet voice. Peace. Peace in spite of expectations, feelings and fears.

James goes on in verse 6, "But when you ask, you must believe and not doubt, because the one who doubts is like a wave of the sea, blown and tossed by the wind."

I must believe God gives wisdom generously. Such confidence underlies the whole process of decision-making. I must believe that peace will come and that God speaks in that peace.

In the case at hand I believe God's will is for me to take on the PTA position. Life is full of surprises. I wonder how it will all look a year from now. But I'm grateful to the Spirit for his peace.

CAN'T BE BOTHERED

"*I* can't stand it any longer! Why don't you take some initiative for a change?" My finger stabbed accusingly at them. "Look at you all! Just like a flock of sheep. Say something!"

Their blank faces stared back at me dispassionately. Then a pretty mouth, ringed with lipstick, slowly opened. "Baaa." The sound, breaking the spell, opened a floodgate. "Baa! Baaaaa!" I blocked my ears and screamed.

Abruptly it was over. I found myself sitting bolt upright in bed soaked in perspiration.

If you have ever been in leadership you will know about apathy. Other people's apathy, that is. It can be so frustrating trying to motivate people. Even worse is being unmotivated yourself. Apathy, indifference, lack of interest, lack of feeling - it's enough to drive anyone over the edge.

Apathy has many causes: protecting myself from repeats of past hurts, a defence against overload, even the result of lack of confidence.

Josie and Cheryl had been attending Diana's Bible study group faithfully for 18 months. They said they enjoyed it and rarely missed, but Diana felt frustrated with both of them. They were so passive and apathetic. She puzzled over the reason. They were so different from each other, yet both so unresponsive.

The orderly ranks of spices and rices marching with military precision across Josie's kitchen cupboards hinted at organisational skills never glimpsed in group functions. She never offered anything much of herself at all. On the other hand, people still talked about Cheryl's dynamic women's ministry. But that was two years ago. Clearly she could relate to people, but she didn't much any more.

Puzzling and praying brought no illumination. So Diana pushed on. Her husband's work took him away from home more and her responsibilities in the church stepped up in pace. After another year she began to wake up with little enthusiasm for the day and very little feeling for others. She felt as wooden as the kitchen table she ate from. What a shock when she finally looked into the mirror over her toothbrush and admitted she didn't care if the women's group folded, Sunday school was cancelled, or a nuclear bomb dropped tomorrow. Apathy.

Both Josie and Cheryl appeared in a different light. How remarkable they'd mustered up the energy to keep coming to Bible study at all if they felt like she did!

Being graced with directness and honesty, Diana sought support and insight quickly. Over a few weeks she realised she was over-stressed. She'd known that had but pushed on believing she could handle it. Now she accepted that overload took its toll on her, as on everyone. Her apathetic state was the result. She needed to make some changes. By listening to her early warning system she averted a more serious slide into depression. She never allowed her unresponsiveness to become a habit.

For three months Diana stopped reading newspapers and avoided TV news. She cut out non-essential meetings and forced herself to spend 15 minutes per day sitting down listening to her favourite worship tapes. After a while she began to feel some emotional response to God again. She began to feel for the joy of feeling.

Over coffee with Josie it struck her that this passive lady only needed permission to do more in the women's group. Josie lacked confidence to take the initiative. Diana shared her struggles and asked Josie to take on organisation of the group. What a change!

Over the next months Josie blossomed. No-one saw her as apathetic again.

Without a green light from the leader, Josie's unused capacities sat idle. Diana began to wonder if her enthusiasm for leading had forced people like Josie into apparent apathy.

Josie first discerned the pain in Cheryl. Through a brief phone interaction about the Christmas break-up, Josie registered Cheryl's pessimism about people. Further contact unfolded a story of hurt in relationships. Years of disappointments in women's ministry had left Cheryl with a legacy of ongoing discouragement. Withdrawal promised safety, protection against more of the same.

Apathy is self-protective. You can't be hurt if you don't feel. "A rock feels no pain and an island never cries." And you can't be disappointed if you never cared in the first place. Pain will lead to hardness, and hardness soon looks like apathy.

Hurt and disappointment plug us up like a blocked drain. The same is true of weariness. When self-preoccupation is blocking natural responsiveness I need the Holy Spirit to release the obstruction. Jesus promised living water to wash us through and flow out of us (John 7:37-39). Paul prayed for the Ephesians to have the mighty inner strengthening of God's Holy Spirit and so experience how long, wide, deep and high God's love is (Ephesians 3:16,19).

A recurring picture in scripture is of people filled up and overflowing. If the outflow has stopped we need God to reveal and remove the pain or fear plugging us up.

Next time you look in the mirror, what will you see? Wink at yourself, and remember you were made to be a confident, responsive and initiating human being.

FEELINGS AND PASSIONS

BOILING OVER

One summer we had a great holiday in southern California, Arizona, Utah and Nevada. Long days driving across the desert made me grateful for our air-conditioned car. On the return journey we decided to drive through the notorious Death Valley. Other friends with children had done it in mid-summer without mishap. And it was the most direct route home. Who could resist such an adventure?

Beautiful, desolate expanses stretched in every direction as we descended below sea level into oppressive heat. To spare the engine we switched off the air-conditioner and sweltered. Our car thermometer showed the temperature outside peaking at 128°F (53°C).

We rarely have radiator problems with our faithful old minivan, but it started to overheat as soon as we began climbing out of the valley. Pretty soon we had to stop, water bubbling from the overflow hose.

Childhood pictures flooded over me. The cars my father drove were always old bombs and I can see him in his overalls bending over the radiator, pouring in water. We've followed in his footsteps so I'm familiar with the experience, too. You have to stop when the radiator boils over. And before you take the cap off, you have to let the radiator cool down or boiling water will spray everywhere.

Then you need to start the engine before you replenish the water or you'll crack the head.

After cooking in Death Valley while our radiator slowly cooled, we were more careful. The gauge told us when the temperature was getting too high and we stopped before it boiled over again. Fortunately there were roadside stops with water tanks at regular intervals. One of them even boasted a hose, and a sign suggesting we spray the front of the radiator while the engine was still running. My husband tried it and the temperature dropped to normal almost immediately. I wondered how Dad never discovered this simple solution.

The rest of our climb out of the valley was punctuated by enforced stops. My husband would race to the front of the car and squirt water from plastic drinking bottles over the radiator. Then back into the car and off again until the next stop. We finally emerged into the shadow of the Sierra Nevada mountains with quite a sense of accomplishment and adventure.

Now in the cool of spring, that day in Death Valley makes me think about anger, emotional radiators and boiling over. I'm struck by a number of parallels between us and the car.

Firstly, some people are more prone to boiling over than others, but anyone is capable of it. (Unlike cars, with people it's not necessarily the older ones who do it more!)

Secondly, boiling or overheating significantly interrupts progress on the journey. Life is delayed and interrupted by anger. We're not very effective when fuming.

A sophisticated temperature gauge is important. Older cars only had a red light. By the time the light came on, you were in trouble. Similarly, some people are surprised and overwhelmed by anger. Today's increased emphasis on communication and expressing how you feel does at least give greater opportunity to avoid that problem. Even if you have an effective gauge, of course, you can still be caught unawares if you don't pay attention to it.

God has equipped us with emotional temperature gauges. But we don't always pay attention to the warning signs. Significant delays from anger are the result. Fast breathing and faster movements; critical, resentful thoughts; preoccupation with a frustrating person or situation; short-tempered reactions to people around us. These are things we should pay attention to.

In Death Valley it was less disruptive to stop and spray down the radiator when warning signs developed than to boil over and wait in the heat. So it is with our personal lives. Even in serious over-heating situations, it's far better to be more aware and take frequent corrective action than to wait for major boilovers that incapacitate you for a long time.

As an aside, we learnt a new solution that my parents didn't know. God can teach us new responses to anger, too. It isn't necessary to be caught in destructive family patterns.

Like a car engine, I would like my emotions to run smoothly and coolly. The challenge is to recognise the warning signals of anger and take corrective action. What serves as water pouring over my soul when I'm overheating? Show me, please, Lord! I need to know or I'll waste my time stuck by the roadside in Death Valley.

JEALOUSY

*A*lmost everyone reading this would have seen the movie *The Sound of Music*. Remember the beautiful, elegant baroness? When she first meets the children she seems enchanted with their singing. Later that evening the children, supported by Maria, plead with their father to sing for them. Clearly, the captain is becoming aware of the freshness and vitality of the attractive young governess who has returned music and laughter to the household. As the guitar passes into the captain's hands, the baroness turns to Max and says, "You should have warned me, darling. I would have brought my harmonica."

A clever comment, smoothly delivered; but a snide one. Suddenly the baroness appears very differently. Her beautifully coiffured hair, impeccable dress and wonderful figure remain the same, but she is ugly. The green-eyed cat of jealousy has showed its claws.

It's so easy to be clever and entertaining but ugly. Much of the smooth, witty talk that goes on in social contact is at the expense of someone and often motivated by jealousy. It seems that deep in the human spirit is a drive to run down others in order to bolster our own self-worth. Is it an attempt to dull the pain of our sense of unworthiness?

The longing for a sense of worth is a need in the human personality. It is an initial design feature and simply will not be denied. Like the need for love, the need for worth must be met somehow. If we desperately need a sense of worth and we equate worth with particular qualities and abilities, then it seems a natural corollary that we will be jealous of those who possess them in greater measure than we do.

Frank's older brother Jim always seemed to shine in whatever he did. Teachers warmed to his open, friendly manner and his natural ability. He was always chosen for special roles in groups and he did well at football. Frank grew up very much in his shadow. It was hard not to feel jealous of Jim's success, and it didn't go away when they grew up and established their own separate lives. Although Frank himself became a successful lawyer, he couldn't stop himself from making snide remarks at family gatherings. Always in fun, of course. His ability with words readily veered towards Jim and his choice of wife, home and occupation, and there was a sting in the cleverness. Whereas Frank felt basically comfortable with himself most of the time, in Jim's presence he felt an awkward, inadequate schoolboy inside. Other people who resembled Jim evoked echoes of the same response. This jealousy was eating away at the fabric of Frank's being, and he knew it.

Because most of us derive our basic nurture and supply from our parents, it is most natural that the earliest messages about our worth come from them. In our natural state we are all driven to draw security and worth from our parents' regard for us. Thus in a sense we are naturally in a state of competition with brothers, sisters and others, too, for our fair share of parental regard. The matter is, of course, more complex, and parents cannot be blamed for all personality weaknesses and struggles with uglies like jealousy! However, the older I get the more I am convinced that jealousy is often deeply entangled with the complexities of sibling rivalry. It carries down from generation to generation.

Jealousy eats you from the inside out. It creates deep inner tension and robs you of joy, especially joy in relationships.

1 John 3:1 says, "How great is the love the Father has lavished on us that we should be called children of God. And that is what we are!" The incredible gospel news is that God loves us and becomes

our Father - true Father, eternal Father. He has the power to heal the inadequacies of human parenting and substitute his eternal secure love and sense of worth for the void within us. This is the foundation for the cure of jealousy.

Much quoted and loved is 2 Corinthians 5:17: "If anyone is in Christ, there is a new creation: the old has gone, the new has come!" This applies with great power to jealousy because it addresses the central emotional issue of worth. God can set us free from our old methods of seeking worth because he gives us worth by sovereign decree.

Frank will not be whole until he experiences the grace of God, and knows him as the Father who loves him; the Father in whose eyes he stands secure and complete in Jesus. This truth must override the low, inadequate view that a jealous person has of himself. This is my prayer for the Franks of the world and indeed for us all. Then the process of relearning and retraining thoughts must go on. By the time jealousy is a conscious problem to be tackled it is a well-ingrained habit. Those habitual jealous thoughts must be doggedly pursued and put down. It's a long battle usually, but freedom can come. It does happen! When you feel jealousy rising in you, respond by lifting up your parents and brothers and sisters to God and asking for his love to wash over you again.

DISAPPOINTMENT

⌘

For several weeks after moving to the United States, I cruised garage sales searching for a pantry cupboard. I furnished our empty house as economically as possible, but not a single pantry cupboard was ever sighted, new or used, except one from a huge warehouse south of where we lived. It was $80 and needed assembly. After weeks of searching I decided to pay the $80. It was hot and the children were very tired of being dragged around shopping, so I set off after my husband came home from work.

It was my first time alone on the freeway, but I made it to the store. After taking ages to get the cupboard I discovered at the checkout that they wouldn't accept my cheque. It needed our name and address printed on it (of course our new personalised ones were still in the mail). Or a local driver's licence would have done it (that was in the mail, too). So I had to leave without the cupboard.

I stewed over it all the way home - it was my fault and I should have planned better. By now it was dark and I suddenly noticed an 'engine warning' light flashing at me on the dashboard. Then I took the wrong turn off the freeway. Here I was, a woman alone at night in a new country, driving along unfamiliar streets in a car that might break down at any moment. And it was all for nothing!

I made it home safely, praise the Lord! But I was very disappointed. I'd been praying about this cupboard. Why had God let it happen?

Sometimes there's an obvious answer to that question and sometimes not. I've met a friend here who is an artist, a professional weaver. Lately she's been working late on a commissioned piece that's overdue. In her tiredness she found she'd made an error towards the end of one panel. It was very disappointing. As she began the weary process of correcting it, she discovered a previous error she'd overlooked. If that panel had been finished and taken off the loom the first error would have been unfixable. For my friend the disappointment led to a blessing. It was easy to see the point in it.

Since my evening jaunt to the warehouse I feel differently about the cupboard. I've realised it wasn't quite right for the kitchen and now it seems a mercy that I couldn't get it. More importantly, being forced to wait has helped restore my perspective about what really matters. At the moment our food is stored in three empty packing boxes stacked sideways on top of each other, but I'm sure the Lord will send a perfect, cheap cupboard to the door ... eventually.

Sometimes what begins as disappointment proves to be God's way of covering our errors or directing us. But it isn't always like that. Some of life's greatest and most meaningless disappointments stem from the choices of others that are beyond our control.

Pantry cupboards are just the tip of the iceberg; a trivial example alongside disappointments in more significant realms. Anyone you meet will carry disappointments tucked away inside. Maybe your spouse hasn't been as understanding as you'd hoped, or your teenager is heading in a direction you wouldn't have chosen, or your friendships haven't developed, or your career options are closing in or even closing down. Life throws up so many disappointments, large and small.

No-one can answer all the 'whys' this side of heaven. But we have one outstanding challenge: to remain soft and open, not hard, in the wake of disappointments. This is the only way consistent with faith. God is our Father, and he keeps every promise he makes. Like a bright lantern in a blackout is the promise of Romans 8:28:

"In all things God works for the good of those who love him and are called according to his purpose."

God's working may be directed more at our beings than our situation. In 1 Peter 5:10, Peter speaks of God himself restoring us and making us "strong, firm and steadfast" after suffering a little.

So there is a deeper kind of work God does in us through disappointment if we yield to him.

As we hang on to him more tightly and look to him more intently to see his work in a situation that doesn't make sense, we get to know him better. He wants to be known, to demonstrate his incredible redemptive power. He is dynamically present, involved in our lives. If we yield our disappointments actively to him, we see him, his creativity, and his faithfulness more fully. We focus on him, and so disappointments become a path to deeper joy.

IT MAKES ME SO MAD

*J*ill had been saving money carefully for months out of her shopping budget to get a new freezer. At last she had enough. She allowed herself to look at the junk mail from electrical stores over her morning coffee. Then, that very week, her son backed into the neighbours' fence and all her savings were needed for repairs.

Jill felt frustrated. In fact, she felt angry. And the whole family knew about it.

She didn't kick the door or yell. It wasn't her way. But the rest of the family stayed well clear that week.

Frustration and anger come from being blocked from some goal we're pursuing. For Jill, the goal and the blockage were clear. Often they're more subtle. John's temper keeps fouling up his image as the super-coping father. Mandy's boisterous two-year-old prevents her living in an atmosphere of order and presenting a composed face to the world.

Are we taken by surprise at our own anger? Do we know what goals drive us? They're deep-seated. To find them we need to do some excavation, to uncover our assumptions about who we are and who we need to be to count as human beings.

Why am I so infuriated at the long queue at the checkout just when I'm running late for the school pickup? Because the children don't like me being late and I hate having a reputation as the late mum. Why is it infuriating to be the late mum? Because it makes me feel incompetent and disorganised. Why is it infuriating to feel incompetent and disorganised? Because worthwhile grown-up people make maximum use of every moment.

And I would be if not for that stupid woman in front with the unpriced item. Why don't people choose items with the price clearly marked? Then I could feel like the super-organised and competent woman that I really am. I must feel that way or I won't fulfil the purpose God made me for. My life won't amount to much. One of my key, deep-seated beliefs about what makes a person worthwhile is hanging right out here.

The spiralling effect of anger is a killer, too. Driving to school muttering to myself about the stupidity of people at checkouts and mothers cramming too much into afternoons and the frequency of red lights will produce all the bodily reactions of stress. My heart will go faster, my breathing will speed up and my thoughts will be quicker and less productive. This is not likely to make me warm, poised and responsive to tired, grumpy children. After a few terse interactions with them, I feel even more a failure as a mother and as a person. They get snitchier with each other, and the spiral goes on.

What goals are you trying to reach? Which blockages consistently tip you over into anger? To begin to change you need to dig up those goals. Focus on them first, because they're inside you. The blockages are often outside you and less under your control.

For me, the goals so often boil down to an image of a worthwhile, valuable woman. While my personal security depends on measuring up to that image of a competent, gracious, effective mother, while I need to prove myself, I set myself up for anger. There will always be blockages in the way.

The strong grace of God's love and forgiveness means we have nothing to fear from our failures. We shouldn't be surprised that we're inadequate. That's part of the basic message of the Bible. God's life flowing through us and his love and forgiveness are incredibly powerful to turn that around.

Life is full of hitches and hold-ups. God has enough ideas and wisdom to give me new strategies. I can learn to factor this reality in, to allow time for delays and interruptions. But first I must be freed from the paralysing effect of anger. The madder I get, the less effective I am. I must loosen my grip on my underlying self-image and the goals that go with it. While my security and worth are vested there, I set myself up. I give the inevitable roadblocks in my life much greater power over me.

The Holy Spirit is expert at loosening my grip on my self-image and fastening my security on Jesus. It's part of his job specification. He's in the business of building a new me. But I have to let him do it. I have to yield my anger to his intervention. That's the way to freedom.

DISCOURAGEMENT

Only yesterday I heard it said that Satan's chief weapon is discouragement. And I know from experience how effectively he can use it. Have you ever prayed for something for a long time, but nothing has changed? Even though there's no evidence that God won't answer, at times it just seems so long and you get tired of waiting.

There have been occasions when I've been involved with someone, and poured myself out in the belief that God is working towards a certain end. Yet no movement happens. I've spoken words of comfort and forgiveness to a defeated friend, only to find them coming back defeated again the next day. After many such cycles it can feel so pointless. Why bother?

When my children are grumpy, irritable and selfish I don't always get warm feelings contemplating the enormous cost of becoming a mother. After all I've put aside to focus on them, where's the fruit?

And what about your extra efforts at work? Does anyone notice or appreciate, or do they just listen to the back-biting about you when you're out of earshot? Many of us carry a load of amorphous discouragement: the worn-down posture of those weary with the dailiness of life.

I'm learning I need to do some rethinking when I experience

this weariness and discouragement. Sometimes I'm simply on the wrong track. Or it may be a matter of perspective. Very often it has to do with perseverance.

Discouragement, like many other unpleasant experiences, affords an opportunity for reassessment. If you're struggling with discouragement, maybe you should take stock of the track you are on. Take the example of caring relationships in a church body. You've struggled to be open, giving and encouraging to people in a home group. It's taken its toll on you and yet little seems to change in their pain and brokenness.

Perhaps the Lord wants you to approach it differently. You strive to match your mind's picture of how a loving Christian should be. The goal is great, but maybe the expression of that aspiration needs to change. Where does your responsibility for someone end and their responsibility for themselves begin? Does your way of showing acceptance actually allow others to build a more stable comfort zone in which to hang on to their destructive behaviour?

In the area of parenting, could the real problem be your expectations of the children? With younger children, very often you'll get what you confidently expect and consistently model to them. Maybe the household schedule is too rigid or too loose. If you're beating your head against a brick wall, stop beating and take a closer look at the wall.

On the issue of perspective, we must always struggle to remind ourselves of eternity. God lives there, and in reality so do we. It just doesn't feel that way. God sent Jacob and his family to Egypt to build them into a nation. There were many generations who lived during the 430 years that it took to do that. No great developments are recorded within that time. Many Israelites had probably lost sight of God's nature and purposes in the daily grind of life. We aren't immune, either; it's almost 2000 years since Jesus lived on earth. He said he was coming back, but it's so easy to get discouraged and lose sight of that reality. It's been so long.

This matter of perspective flows over into the third issue of perseverance. If we use discouragement to pause and reassess, God may show us a different tack to take. But he may confirm the tack we're on and just tell us to get on with it.

Exodus 5 shows Moses at a point of great discouragement. After an incredible meeting with God at the burning bush, he has been sent back to Egypt where the Israelites have received him and experienced a revival in worship as a result. But after Moses' first contact with Pharaoh, things get worse rather than better. Instead of letting the people go, Pharaoh increases their workload by forcing them to gather their own straw to make bricks. The Israelites turn on Moses in anger and the whole situation looks very bleak.

His response? He turns to God and asks two questions: "Why have you brought trouble on these people? Is this why you sent me?" (Exodus 5:22). Discouragement is meant to drive us to the Lord, not away. Moses received a great affirmation of his calling and a great promise from God. Trouble was still to come and Moses was miserable, but he wasn't wrong. He was doing God's will in an evil world, and sometimes that involves discouragement.

Are you weary of well-doing, discouraged from doing God's will in an evil world? Don't give up! There's a great promise in Galatians 6:7-9. It opens with a warning, but it goes on to assure us that "the one who sows to please the Spirit, from the Spirit will reap eternal life. Let us not become weary in doing good, for at the proper time we will reap a harvest if we do not give up." What a promise! We can ask the Lord to give us a little rest or a change when we need it, but let's not allow discouragement to put us out of the race.

JOURNEYING FROM LONELINESS
TO RELATIONSHIP

$\iff$

*W*hen it comes to overcoming emotional struggles and living a real life, 'how-to' articles often seem trite. They make it sound too easy. Printed words cannot be a hug.

Nevertheless, try to imagine a luscious pavlova. A photo of one might be tantalising, but if I want to make one, I need a recipe. This article offers a recipe for moving from loneliness to relationship, with the main ingredients being honesty, initiative and perseverance.

Honesty, when tempered with gentleness, is beautiful. A major component of honesty is self-disclosure. Indeed, self-disclosure is the basic ingredient of closeness, whereas loneliness is related to an unwillingness or inability to share one's inner self.

We hold back because we are ashamed of our weaknesses. Yet forgiven people no longer need fear their own failures and weaknesses; they stand on the foundation of God's acceptance, whatever rejection and failure come their way. We thrill to this truth in theory. Why, then, do we scurry for cover whenever an actual weakness pops out?

When Sally was stressed, she became gruff and harboured critical thoughts. At the last women's ministry team meeting, when Joan started about the group's narrow approach to outreach, Sally had let slip a sharp retort.

On reflection later that night, she felt convinced that Joan's comments, though they held some truth, were by no means the whole picture. She had a sneaking suspicion that Joan was rather proud of her insightful challenges. But she still felt uncomfortable about her own behaviour. She resolved to call on Joan the next day.

Sally had two choices of approach. She could justify herself, accounting for her sharpness by her stressed, tired state, or she could wholeheartedly apologise for her own critical approach, calling it what it was.

Joan is far more likely to warm to the latter. Vulnerability begets vulnerability, which leads to closeness. However, vulnerability requires courageous honesty. It is an act of faith in the forgiveness and faithfulness of God. Few words in the English language are more powerful in building bridges than "I'm sorry".

Honesty does more than reveal weakness. For people to know me, I must reveal my thoughts, my likes and dislikes, my ways of having fun, of relaxing, of showing tiredness, and so on. I draw closer to people by expressing appreciation, too.

One key to self-disclosure is story-telling. This leads to the second ingredient: initiative. Initiative is important for everyone, not just extroverts. To come close, you must contribute something of yourself, and a great way to do that is by telling stories of your experience. I don't mean like those boring, dominating people who go on and on about themselves. It's such a pleasure to be in the company of someone who thoughtfully observes life and selects a subset of experience to share because it might especially interest you.

Mothers do this automatically. I remember interrupting a serious conversation in my car by crying out, "Look, two fire engines!", only to remember there were no children present at the time. My friends had a good laugh. Looking for trucks and fire engines was a habit—one I certainly didn't have before I had sons.

What is the equivalent for the people in your world? Could you put a newspaper cutting in a colleague's pigeonhole at work? Or invite a neighbour over to show her your azaleas or the quilt you've completed?

Talk of initiative leads to the third ingredient: perseverance. Real life involves disappointments, and if you dare to reach out to others, you'll meet some. All I can say is persevere. It is actually possible to live through the sting of rejection. Is God your Father a strong, resilient God who has got hold of you to make you strong and resilient, too? Or do you want to remain a tender bloom sheltered from sun, rain and wind forever? Shrinking from short-term pain may lead to deeper wounds in the long term.

May the God of all grace give you his grace and strength.

WEEDING IS NO GOOD UNLESS
YOU GET OUT THE ROOTS

ithout being a gardener, I find great pleasure pottering in my garden. Oh, the satisfaction of a weed coming out as I yank it, roots and all. It's no good pulling out most of a weed. You have to get the roots.

I can't help being spiritual in my garden, and weeds make me think about sin. Sin is more than an assortment of actions obvious on the surface of our lives. It is something rooted much more deeply in our personalities.

One sunny day as I tackled a whole lot of nutweed in our backyard I was struck by the complex network of tiny threads under the ground connecting all the roots. Each weed was not an individual, but an expression of the whole weed system permeating the soil. Sin proliferates in my life just as weeds cover the ground. And pride is the hidden root system.

"If you think you are not conceited, it means you are very conceited indeed", wrote CS Lewis in *Mere Christianity*.

Pride sneaks into everything. My highest moments of selfless love, when I am lost in contemplation of another, are very short-lived. Before I know it, I'm proud that I'm capable of such a high and spiritual experience.

Pride distances me from God because it turns the focus on me. This insatiable appetite for admiration, this self-focus is the essential sin, the root system, because it must be at the expense of God who is the true focus. When I am self-absorbed, when I thirst for admiration of myself, I suppress the truth of who God really is.

As the pervasive presence of pride in my being becomes clearer, it is most humbling. But I am not going to let it discourage me. I cannot plumb the depths of my own pride. But Jesus has. He knows the rock bottom of it. I want him to dig out the roots. Sometimes he has to yank.

And it's not painless. Like all of our brokenness, pride is stressful and uncomfortable to live with. It has major consequences in relationships. Is it difficult to forgive hurts? Is there hardness inside when certain people come to mind? Do I stiffen with anger or irritability when others don't take me seriously or recognise my obvious qualities? How do I feel when others are affirmed and praised? Yank, yank, yank. Jesus is busy in these times.

I remember speaking with a woman who worked very hard at doing good. In fact, she was exhausted. When a refreshing wave of new experience of God's love swept through her church, leaving some of her friends overwhelmed, she felt distinctly on the outside. If anyone deserved to feel close to God, surely it was her. But she felt distant. Most of her friends hadn't sacrificed themselves as she had, yet they were obviously experiencing a joy that was missing from her life. In time, she came to realise that it was her pride in her good behaviour and self-sacrifice that stood between her and God. We can unknowingly elevate ourselves to a position in which God is answerable to us.

A dear friend of mine is good at leading public meetings. Recently she had an unusual chance to lead at a series of evenings and she loved it. "I had a ball—each time I seemed to be in the right place at the right time, and God really touched people. Looking back since, I've struggled with the line between joy at being useful to God and pride. My conclusion is that when you do what you're made for, there's a deep satisfaction that isn't pride. It's joy. But it can be spoilt and turned into pride if you let it. On the last occasion as I was preparing to lead, I was praying about this issue of pride. I wanted to be pure. I felt God's response. As I got up to lead I felt so nervous, far more so than before. Without expecting an answer I asked, 'Lord, why am I so nervous tonight?' Immediately, he responded, 'Because I've emptied you of yourself.' I felt such joy. I knew God could do something through me, and he did."

As cholesterol is to arteries, so is pride to the human spirit. It hardens and narrows us. Eventually it blocks off the flow of life completely. We become less spontaneous, more calculated, isolated. Pride cannot laugh at itself. Pride is self-absorption. As God forgives and loves us, he moves us out into a much bigger world. He becomes more and more our focus, our frame of reference.

The first step is acknowledging our pride. An enormous step! Then we need to start laughing at ourselves. As I stop taking myself so seriously I can feel the melting of that cholesterol. I feel the softening of the soil. Every time I inwardly step back and have a chuckle at my self-focused reactions, I feel God yanking. The weeds give way. The ground is softer. The roots come out.

COFFEE WITH ALLAN

"It's your pride", he says,
"and your idealism.
A potent mixture
killing you slowly
from the inside out.
Your heart is a stone within you
because you're not the best.
Not enough.
Give what you are."

This husband of tender ruthlessness.
This man You gave me.

Oh well,
swirling the cup, I
throw the mixture over my shoulder.

Now we'll see
if there is any me
left to pour out.

BEING ANGRY ALL THE TIME
MAKES ME SICK!

o-one likes being around angry people—you keep your distance from the spitfires. And everyone knows who they are. If you live with an angry person you'll know the subtle and complex manoeuvres the family system goes through to contain and avoid anger. It's exhausting, stressful and definitely a health hazard. If anger is a problem for you, you'll have a life strewn with relationships in disarray.

What are we supposed to do with the anger that springs up and grabs us in the gut? How can we change?

Most of us want to avoid the destructiveness of anger when it all hangs out. Who wants to be a spitfire? So lots of us stuff angry feelings down and try to keep the lid on. They can get buried so deeply that we don't even know they're there.

We might not even get it when we're diagnosed with spastic colon or stress-related heart disease.

Or we can know the anger is there but work really hard at keeping the lid on it.

Marian decided she shouldn't get angry as a Christian. If her husband made a comment that hurt her, she would remind herself that Christian wives should be forgiving. When her husband asked her what was wrong, she'd say "Nothing", believing that she should get on top of her sinful anger and be more mature. However, at bedtime when her husband wanted a cuddle, would Marian be responsive? Of course not! The anger was expressed, just not directly. Anger has a way of oozing out somehow.

Julia wasn't exactly a spitfire. She was lovely. But at home she was stewed up at least once a week. She'd race around muttering if she was alone. However much she tried to stop it, her anger and tension would rise as she rehearsed to herself the disrespectful attitude of her children and their laziness around the house. The more she asked them to help, the more they complained about being nagged. Julia felt hurt and annoyed by their behaviour and the family soon learnt when to avoid her. She took headache tablets regularly and often felt like a failure. She had prayed many times to be freed from the cycle. It didn't make for good relationships with her children or her husband. Not to mention the neighbours who once heard her yelling at her son in the backyard—so much for asking them to the church picnic. Julia didn't push her anger down as much as Marian, but she wasn't in a good way.

Expressing feelings directly is so much better than either repressing or suppressing them. That's why counsellors have people thrashing mattresses and pounding pillows, letting it all hang out in the safe environment of a counselling room. Julia and Marian would do much better saying directly what was bugging them.

Expression doesn't give you a better way of handling the tension next time, though. It's essential but not enough.

There's another way, a beautiful way called confession. Confession contains expression, but it's more than that. It carries with it an openness, an acknowledgment of a need to be different, a softness. Repression and suppression are not honest. Expression is honest but not sufficient. I can express angry feelings very intensely while still justifying myself. I am then just as vulnerable to those feelings next time the difficulty arises.

If I express my anger and struggles to a friend or a counsellor and ask for help, there is an element of confession in it. For me, it's even better first to confess to God. The confessing attitude says, "This is how I feel. I neither condemn nor justify myself. I am in your hands, Father God. You alone know when I am the victim and when the perpetrator of wrong. I don't hide from you or myself the anger within me. I believe the cross of Jesus deals with this anger and I ask you to apply the power of Jesus' forgiveness to my reactions in this situation. Take me as I am and shape me as you choose."

You can be as angry as you like in God's presence. He is well able to handle it.

An open, receptive attitude allows reflection on the angry reactions, their causes and how to do better. God and other good friends can really help with new ideas.

Marian and Julia both needed to change to be more honest. Shouting and crying and talking all have their place.

We all need to trust God less from just our head and more from our gut, and expect him to accept us and to actually change us in his own way. He's ready, willing and able.

I'M SO ORDINARY - WHAT DO I
MATTER?

*P*erhaps all writing is cathartic - or at least autobiographical. This piece is certainly so. One of my recurrent struggles is with a sense of ordinariness, mediocrity, not mattering.

Perhaps my reactions are the result of 13 years of mothering and just being tired, but I find the very thought of the information superhighway overwhelming, for example. How can I compute the enormous volume of knowledge available at my fingertips? People all over the world are accessible to me in my own living room via the Internet. The wonder and convenience of telecommunication technology often feels like a burden of responsibility, a pressure of communication all around and on top of me.

When I was a child I loved bookshops and libraries, often running to the school library the minute the recess bell rang. The aisles of a well-lit bookshop still have the lure of a wonderland. And in my memory an aura surrounds the reading room of my university library. How I savoured those delicious years, studying at heavy desks where generations had sat. How I enjoyed the huge room's faded elegance. How imposing the grandeur of years of accumulated scholarship and insight.

But sometimes even these feelings seem overwhelming. I have actually walked out of a Christian bookshop within minutes of entering it because it seems too much. Surely every possible useful thing that could be written about has been written about. How could I think I would ever have anything more to offer? What's the point of adding to the enormous smorgasbord of offerings on the shelves already?

Similar feelings arise in the shopping centre or on the street. There are countless people. I can go out into the same range of places day after day and see different people all the time. Everyday faces I've never seen sit beside my car at the stop light or wait behind me at the supermarket checkout. If I turn on the radio the chances are high I'll be able to find some intelligent person talking about a whole area of knowledge of which I'm completely ignorant.

Surrounded by these throngs, I'm not indispensable. No individual is. Sudden deaths and migrations to other cities and countries bring that vividly home. Life goes on without me.

It's not necessary to respond to this complex world by feeling like a small unimportant dot. But I know I often do. So what is the truth about all of us little dots amongst billions on the face of the earth?

We know that Jesus said (in Luke 12:6,7) that we're of great worth to God. He even knows how many hairs are on my head. That's quite amazing—a good place to start. Apparently our Father in heaven considers each of us five billion dots valuable enough to know us intimately and to notice how many hairs fall onto the bedroom floor when we brush our hair in the morning.

Even the most ordinary things count for something. I remember years ago walking a teenage girl home to her campsite from the coffee tent in which we were holding a Scripture Union Beach Mission. She was staying out of the town with no near neighbours. As I returned to our campsite alone I was struck by the blackness. I hadn't noticed it when talking. There were no streetlights out there and scarcely any moon that night. It was really, really dark. In that situation just one light, even a torch, would have made an enormous difference. Neither one old streetlight nor a torch seems noticeable in the day. They're very ordinary objects.

Along our suburban street the trees grow large and leafy and the streetlights nestle unobtrusively amongst them. At night, though, how important those lights are in the shapeless darkness. If one or two lights are out, the safety and the feel of the whole stretch of street is different. If I were a streetlight I might be tempted to feel unimportant. How would I matter when there are so many others on either side of me? But I would matter.

And, as a person, I do matter. God has put me in one particular spot for his own purpose. No-one else has the job of mothering my children and 'wife-ing' my husband. I am Jesus' presence in my neighbourhood and school community—in my network of friends.

In Philippians 2:15, Paul describes us as shining like stars in the universe as we hold out the word of life. If I don't shine for him where I am, who will? Even the most talented person can't touch the lives around me from a distance. That is my unique charge from God.

EVEN ME

As if Shakespeare never peppered his cabbage.
As if Anne Frank never cleaned sleep from her eyes in the
    morning.
As if Mother Theresa wasn't grumpy ... at least sometimes.

Can not I, formed in middle-class suburbia,
Frittered away by telephone solicitors
and exhaust fumes
and supermarket checkouts,
Grasp the vapours of my soul's eternity
And release some into our room?

Can not I leave the fragrance of His indwelling,
For future tenants,
For my unknown kin?

Prepare us for eternal communion.

Yes
I will spread the petals of my bloom before it is spent,
I will leave what trail I can
Through our home's dark hallways.

Grasp His insistent presence in my mediocrity.

Follow the scent of heaven.

FRESH APPROACHES TO OLD ISSUES

OUT OF FOCUS

"*D*eciding what not to do", smiled Mary. "That's what my father always told me was the secret to success."

Walking my children past the school office towards home, I found myself shoulder-to-shoulder with Mary. She is a vibrant, talented artist with a long grey plait down her back and dancing blue eyes.

"He said to make lists of the things I had to do, cut them in half and just let the bottom half slip away." With a sweep downwards of her right arm, she stepped back as if watching the bottom of her list fall into a black pit. "Selective neglect is the key."

Many thoughts flashed through my mind. *What a great father! ... the tyranny of the urgent ... be prepared to sacrifice the good for the better and the better for the best.*

I thought about the week I was living right then. My husband was away. I had school meetings and welcome picnics to arrange and lead, and school open-house nights to attend. Each event required babysitting arrangements. Then the cooking, shopping, laundry and usual chores always pressed in. All must be fitted around chauffeuring children and supporting them through home-work and their adjustment to a new school grade.

It was a breathless sort of week. Which items on my daily lists should I put on the bottom half and drop into the pit?

Such seasons in life raise issues of stress management. How do we live free of constant suppressed panic? How do we avoid slipping into that groove called 'busy but empty'? In my life these questions have recurred.

God has worked over the years and this particular week has not landed me in panic mode. I know God well enough to know his provision and I know myself well enough to know my panic achieves a fat zero of fruit. No, this week was not about stress-management issues - at least not directly. Rather, I found myself reflecting on focus.

One of the haunting and sapping feelings that busyness brings is being diffused, frittered away.

Is my life poured out by little portions into many receptacles? Lots of me gets poured out. But does the level change substantially in any of the pots? This is a feeling of life being unfocused and dissipated away.

The world doesn't stop and let you off, but I'd like to make three simple suggestions for retaining focus.

Firstly, all life can be a prayer. As I work through my list of errands and make contact with numerous people, I have a choice. I can circulate my own thoughts around my head and my horizontal surroundings, or I can pray for everyone I meet quietly in the recesses of my mind.

An undercurrent of prayer has surprising power to weave the disparate strands of a day into a whole. Such gentle prayer doesn't detract from efficiency. It keeps you constantly breathing the air of eternity amongst the fumes of the world.

Secondly, time out to specifically pray with someone is always time well spent.

It sounds trite. At the beginning of the week I discussed my upcoming days with my husband before he left. Where could I plan better? What could I delete to make the week work? It seemed silly to accept an invitation to pray with two women. Why add something new right now? "I'll cancel that", I thought. But Allan encouraged me to leave that item on the top half of the list. So I learnt again this week the simple lesson that prayer is a first priority. That time drew out of me more real sharing than I expected and opened me to God's presence more deeply. It was time well spent.

Finally, I need to do what makes my heart sing. How do I know what God has specifically made me for? Well, what makes my heart sing? So much time has to be spent on mundane tasks. That's just life. Underpinning them with prayer is important, but there's more. Just half an hour to relate to God in a way that expresses my deep self can carry me through days of 'mundane' busyness.

Perhaps it's dancing or sewing, or playing music to God. Perhaps it's making a meal for someone or making a gift or writing a poem. Expressing yourself in a way that God has uniquely gifted you is renewing. This productivity from deep within pulls your being into focus and guards against diffusion.

"I have come that you might have life and have it to the full", Jesus said. He, who lived so totally clearly, vividly and always in focus, wills the same for us. Let's be willing to selectively neglect the urgent to keep in focus the fruitful.

LOS ALTOS LIBRARY

She stood beside her car
outside the library.
Well into middle years, with a square, heavy face and a
    striped T-shirt.
The library wasn't open yet,
but her compact was.
She examined her face carefully in a tiny mirror
and applied red lipstick with gentle stretches of her mouth.
Why does she bother?
Why would a 65-year-old woman wear bright red lipstick?
And why stand in the open
in public
to put it on?
Two young skinheads drove by
and looked at her blankly.
With a sigh of satisfaction
composed
put together
she put away her lipstick and ambled towards the library
    door.
Inside
shelves are packed with a world's experience.

The cries and whispers of countless
hearts and lips
sit in silent rows there.
Perhaps she will take one
and go home to her own private place
and look carefully
into a mirror for her soul.

CHRISTMAS: FRIEND OR FOE?

❧

"*You* know what you get if you rearrange the letters of Santa, don't you?"

I glanced at my friend, trying to hide my surprise. My thoughts hadn't wandered from our weekly playgroup; hers were obviously far away. Our pre-schoolers ran past, squealing happily.

"This commercialism is just a cover for Satan's work distracting us from Jesus!"

Well, yes, I could certainly harmonise with that sentiment. Each Christmas found me restlessly feeling there must be a better way to celebrate Jesus' coming. In a moment a parade of our regular Christmas season passed through my mind. Dragging around the stores looking for inspiration, not knowing what on earth my brothers might like now they are grown men. Or if pretty stationery would please nieces who had mysteriously turned into sophisticated teenagers. Each year found me wishing that relationships in my wider family were closer so that the gift-giving ritual was more meaningful.

Without a doubt the best part was the Christmas service. Jesus barely rated a mention at my family's Christmas lunch, but how lovely to go early in the morning and sing beautiful carols, awed again that the one who flung the stars into space should come to us. God a little baby in the care of a peasant girl!

As my siblings' families and ours began multiplying, Christmas became more exciting and more complicated. On our turn to host, my husband and I put up signs about Christmas being Jesus' birthday and occasionally prepared craft activities for the children about the nativity. Over the years the gift-giving became streamlined and eventually dwindled away.

In my husband's family the day was more purely joy. The whole wider family is Christian and genuinely finds joy in each other's company. They represent a different approach to Christmas, being sincere believers yet relishing the trappings. We enjoy a wonderful, traditional roast meal with bonbons and the lot and a huge tree piled with presents.

So in a few short seconds I scanned the different approaches to Christmas in my own personal world. Some Christians keep their focus on Jesus but wholeheartedly embrace the trappings of the holiday. Others react to the loss of focus on Jesus and come to hate the secularised, spiritually empty, stressful carry-on—I have a friend who wishes the church would abandon December and have a new, spiritual Christmas at another time. Still others, the majority of our culture, don't give Jesus a moment's thought. They see the day as a time for food, gifts, family time and children. Whether it's a fun day or not depends mostly on the state of family relationships. Any sense of meaning is reduced to sentiment, a sort of vague piety.

I've never forgotten my friend's comments at playgroup. Is Christmas friend or foe? With December again on the horizon, I decided to research Christmas. I've wanted for years to get to the bottom of it. Is it simply a Christian festival, a celebration of the Son of God made flesh? Is it a pagan ritual in disguise, dressed up to hide the truth from its unsuspecting victims? Or is it just a convenient vehicle for unrestrained consumerism?

All these attitudes have historical precedents. Twenty centuries of church life have witnessed waves of response to the festival. How did our Christmas culture develop?

Ancient cultures had feasts tied to the growing season. Egypt, Mesopotamia, Greece and Rome each developed variants on the theme of celebrating life's reappearance on the earth after the barrenness of winter or drought.

At the winter solstice Romans honoured Saturn, the god of agriculture, with Saturnalia. Persians lit fires in praise of Mithra, god of light; for them 25 December was the "birthday of the unconquered sun" and the start of the new year. All midwinter festivals hailed the victory of light and life over darkness and death. And these festivals included gift-giving, evergreen branches, food, merry-making and lights.

Heavily persecuted, the early church kept a low profile on celebration and Jesus' birthday was largely ignored. Its true date was unknown and no instruction to observe it was left by Jesus or any biblical writer.

Then, after centuries of struggle, the Christian church was suddenly 'successful' after Constantine's 313 AD edict. When people gave up pagan gods to worship the true God they were encouraged to mark the rebirth of the year with thanksgiving to their Father God who had sent Jesus. The sun had become the Son.

In 350 AD Pope Julius I set the probable date of Christ's birth as 25 December. Christians have mostly accepted this, knowing it is arbitrary, although some have always disliked a time so close to pagan holidays.

Perhaps the newly legal Christians wanted to placate the devotees of Mithra (a popular cult in the Roman legions). A festival on the day most sacred to Mithra might provide a bridge over which sun worshippers could cross.

The trouble with bridges, of course, is that traffic can go both ways. This two-way traffic is precisely the struggle that has exercised the church down through the centuries.

All manner of wild celebrations became attached to Christmas at various stages. The third century Christian scholar Origen decried celebrating Christ's birthday as though he were a king pharaoh. In 575 Bishop Martin of Bracae in Germany forbade Christmas evergreens as a dangerous heathen custom; they didn't reappear in churches for centuries.

Celebration of Christmas was outlawed in Cromwell's puritan England. In 1656, Hezekiah Woodward thoroughly denounced it, using terms like "the profane man's ranting day, the superstitious man's idol day, Satan's working day ... we are persuaded no one thing more hindereth the Gospel work all year long than doth the observation of that idol day, once a year, having so many days of cursed observation with it." Serious words indeed!

All these statements can only be rightly assessed in their cultural contexts (too much to do here), but our friends who would like to abandon Christmas have had supporters down the centuries.

So the celebration was based on ancient pagan customs and resisted for centuries by early Christians. Then, as still more centuries passed, it was 'christianised'. Some elements of the ancient festivities have fallen away. Others lend themselves to new meaning. Evergreen leaves as a picture of everlasting life can readily evoke thoughts of Jesus. (Christmas trees are a relatively recent addition, only 300 years old.) The Roman candles of Saturnalia are easily seen as symbols of the true light of the world. Exchanging gifts is a vivid reminder of wise men's gifts and, more importantly, God's gift of Jesus.

Times of spiritual renewal have produced wonderful additions to the celebrations. Francis of Assisi in 1223, by asking for a live re-enactment of the nativity, released a beautiful and enduring element of Christmas, the nativity scene. One of his Franciscans (Jacopone da Todi), a songwriter and poet, is credited with the "first real outburst of Christmas joy in a popular tongue". Over the 700 years since, a most wonderful flow of music has both presented and praised the Jesus of Bethlehem. Masterpieces have been painted on the theme, and renaissance madonnas are still popularly associated with Christmas via cards.

Should we shun Christmas like Cromwell, or christianise it like da Todi? One thing emerged clearly during my reading: each generation of Christians must evaluate the culture it finds itself in and form its own responses.

In our culture Christmas is perceived as a Christian celebration, not connected in the public mind to pagan rituals. When we talk about putting the "Christ back into Christmas" it makes sense to our contemporaries, even if they aren't sympathetic.

But since most people don't know Jesus in a dynamic way, the spiritual thrust of a festival like Christmas will inevitably be drained. We can choose our response to this loss of focus on Jesus. We can say the traffic across the bridge is mostly in the wrong direction and try to blow it up. Or we can see an opportunity to reverse the flow.

Are the pagan roots of the festival our real enemy at Christmas? Paul's discussion (1 Corinthians 8:4-9) of meat offered to idols and our freedom in Christ assures me there is no spiritual power over me in the ancient, pagan origins of many Christmas trappings. In themselves they are not to be feared.

Of more concern is the frenzied, headlong march into materialism. We've moved from worship of Saturn and Mithras to worship of the great god Mammon.

The older I get the more distressed I become about the commercialism. And I know I am not alone. We must see our enemies—commercialism and sentimentalism—for the spiritual forces they are. We must prayerfully resist.

We can take positive initiatives with our children. We can talk about the wonder of Jesus' coming, the events of his birth, who he is and how very happy we are about him. Life without festive punctuation in the work routine would be sorry indeed and, since we find ourselves in a culture that celebrates Christmas, why not make the most of it?

Our family principle is to select carefully the subset of activities we engage in and do what relates to Jesus in a meaningful way. See the accompanying "Winning Christmas Back".

Apart from celebrating with children, Christmas yields great opportunities for communicating the gospel. My cycle of frustration, feeling trapped into empty, secular traditions, yet loving the heart of it, has given way to peace. In 1 Corinthians 9:22, Paul wrote about using all means to bring salvation to people. Because centuries of Christian overlay on the pagan rituals have significantly changed them, the festive season now presents the church with wonderful evangelistic openings.

What other time of year lends itself so readily to sharing God's undeserved love with those who don't know him? What other time of year finds people who normally never darken the door of a church so open to invitation? December is a time for acts of compassion and creative evangelistic thrust.

Christmas is not sacred. It is not baptism or communion. But it offers a lovely reason to celebrate. Children relate to birthdays. Let's rejoice with creativity and gusto. Let's refocus on Jesus and talk with the children about him as we bake and sing, draw and dance, decorate and give gifts. Let's also make sure we give to the needy in the name of Jesus and put our very best efforts into communicating the gospel to our neighbours in the day of opportunity.

We pray our family's Christmas activities will be a bridge over which the traffic flows to Jesus and some glimmer of his brilliance shines into the lives around us. Let it be so, Lord Jesus!

WINNING CHRISTMAS BACK

⚜

*C*elebrations are supposed to be fun and we want Christmas to draw us closer to Jesus. This is our family's how-to for Christmas as it has evolved so far.

Food

While there is nothing sacred about the traditional roast, and some drawbacks in Australian Christmas weather, there's nothing wrong with it either. Perhaps in our country the festive fare will change over generations to come, but lots of people would still miss their turkey and chicken if it wasn't served. When baking extras like biscuits, I stick to symbols that relate to Christ—stars and angels—avoiding reindeer, candy canes and the like.

Decorations

A green tree with decorations is a lovely sight and provides harmless fun for children. Our goal is to collect ornaments over the years that speak of Jesus. We skip snowy scenes, cute creatures or elves in favour of ornaments that speak about Jesus' identity or the nativity. The Lutherans have given us 'chrismons', ornaments you can make out of polystyrene, beads and glue (Bible bookshops often sell instruction books). We've enjoyed a number of afternoons with family friends making these beautiful symbols of Jesus. It's a golden opportunity to talk with children about God's plan and the names of Jesus.

Candles point to him as the light of the world.

We decorate the house simply, focusing on the nativity. Our focal point is a simple, white nativity set surrounded by a ring of green leaves with lights in them. The tree takes a lesser place. The walls are covered with children's nativity drawings, birthday banners for Jesus and my home-made attempts at attention-catching sayings like "Wise men seek him still".

MUSIC

Music is always a high point of the season. Carols and contemporary Christmas music evoke great joy and can powerfully present the gospel.

Many of the traditional winter references make no sense at all in Australia. Children sing about jingling bells and open sleighs dashing through the snow, all in the heat of an Australian summer. How that relates to God sending his Son into the world is beyond me! There are so many other wonderful things to sing about.

It has given me great joy to develop and present Christmas dances at church. Our daughters love taking part. What marvellous Christmas memories, too! Randy Stonehill's evergreen *Christmas Song* and Cliff Richard's *Saviour's Day* have been powerful and satisfying for the purpose.

Singing, dancing or playing are all great family activities at home. But if none of that fits you, how about baking, sewing or drawing with the children? Most people enjoy constructing a nativity scene and the range of possible materials is huge. Let's produce a creative response to the Christmas story each year and have fun doing it together.

Cards

The first Christmas card appeared in England in 1843. It's lovely to hear from friends but there's nothing sacred about sending cards. Since the children arrived I just haven't managed it regularly. Again, it's good to keep the focus on Jesus and remember to use the greetings to glorify him. We choose nativity scenes rather than trees, mistletoe and elves. Many Christians make their own. Could this be the creative project for you and the children this year?

Presents

What joy to give gifts to our children! And what a worry that we're just reinforcing their self-centredness. Each year we try to simplify what we buy but it isn't easy to find the balance. It would be too sad and stark to have no gifts, so we enjoy giving each child three gifts (not very big) and talk a lot about Jesus being the best gift of all. "Yes ... yes", say their eyes, "but let's get on with the other presents!" We live in hope of God's voice through the memories of joy.

Along with family presents there must be giving to the poor. Many charities, and surely all churches, use Christmas as an opportunity to reach out to the needy. We choose one or two avenues and communicate with the children about it. Personal involvement through volunteering time or visiting people is even better.

And we can't talk about presents without talking about ...

Santa

Allan and I both grew up with Father Christmas, one in a Christian home and one not. We both enjoyed it and came to no harm in our relationships with either parents or God. Some people do find their disillusionment about him traumatic. However, given our experience we planned to include Santa without making a big deal of him.

Then we had children. Making the effort to create the illusion proved surprisingly unappealing. It felt like lying to the children and we couldn't see any reason to do so.

So Santa missed out. When the children were old enough to notice him in stores we simply explained he is part of the tradition of Christmas but not connected to Jesus being born. Sure, it's exciting to think of some great mysterious figure who watches us and gives us presents. However, we know God our Father who loves and watches over us and gives us so much. At Christmas we especially celebrate that he gave us Jesus.

We impressed upon the children the importance of not upsetting other children by saying Father Christmas isn't true. Let the parents handle that. So far, we don't know of our children offending or upsetting anyone, and with our youngest now eight we're probably out of the woods.

We feel no desire to campaign against Santa. But we've never taken the children to a store to see one, either. If a Santa appears at a work function, the children just accept the gifts gratefully.

Our family practice has been to put a small stocking on each bed to be found in the morning. They contain things like a marker, some lifesavers, a pretty ink stamp and a pack of collectable cards. The children know we're responsible, not Father Christmas, but their pleasure seems undiminished.

How did the modern Santa evolve? In ancient times a European pagan goddess of fire and the hearth was held to visit homes secretly in mid-winter. She was Berchta—sometimes kindly, but often portrayed as a witch-like figure. She brought rewards for goodness; an elf-like creature accompanied her who punished bad behaviour.

St Nicholas, the saintly bishop of Myra in Turkey, lived in the late fourth century. He was kind and compassionate and stories grew up after his death about his acts of giving. These merged with the Berchta legends, and the secret Christmas visitor became St Nicholas. By the 18th century the St Nicholas tradition was complete in Europe.

In the US, a new wave of interest was sparked in 1822 when Clement Clarke Moore wrote a poem for his six young children: *The Night before Christmas*. This St Nicholas had a sleigh and reindeer. Illustrations in the *Harper's Weekly* over 23 years and then a series of Santa drawings for Coca-Cola's December campaigns in 1931 completed a new picture.

Gone was the saintly bishop. The new Santa was robust, grandfatherly and over six feet tall, with elves as helpers in producing toys. America's St Nicholas was as different from Europe's as the new world from the old.

After World War II, American GIs held parties for children all over Europe and their kindness made the American Santa widely known. Hence Father Christmas as we know him.

Incorporating him into a spiritually meaningful Christmas requires too much contortion for us. And he is an easy access point for the power of commercialism. These are our family views—we have no chapter and verse—and each family must be free to find its own pattern directed by the Spirit. We're all aiming for the same goal: to give joy and to celebrate Jesus.

Festive gathering

Festivals are social. It wouldn't be Christmas without the company of those we love. Let's just remember to praise Jesus when we get together. Special church services and Bible reading and singing in the home are simple and powerful ways to do that. It moved me last year to hear the nativity story read from scripture in our home group by the children.

The other main thrust is sharing God's love. Can you be sure to include at least one Christmas event on the calendar for reaching out? Last year we went carol singing with friends from church, handing out a little gift (biscuits) and a statement about God's love to each household.

For the last three years I have invited mothers from the children's school to a Christmas coffee morning. This year I plan to include a short talk on the true meaning of Christmas. In our church we hope to have a series of these in homes this December.

One year my husband and two other men from our home group dressed up as wise men and went to the local shopping centre giving out little bags of sweets with a simple gospel message. The rest of us prayed. They had great fun and said it was very well received.

There are endless possibilities and joys as we all focus on Jesus and gradually reshape our celebration of Christmas to truly glorify him.

FINDING DE GATE IN DE FENCE

*lancing across the assembled wedding guests enjoying their festive dinner, my gaze came to rest on my friend's profile. She looked lovely tonight—her dark hair streaming down her back, her eyes and lips glowing. She always could wear that bright red lipstick. I never had the courage. A quiver ran through me. As I watched her laugh and chat with first this group and then that, I felt a distinct space between us. A little pang around my heart. What had she been thinking about me lately?

I found myself remembering our recent ministry review. My friend had asked for honest feedback about our leadership team. And I had given it, despite initial hesitations. Sharing some of my personal struggles in the team relationships proved more of a relief than I expected. She seemed open and appeared to receive it graciously.

But next time we met she was angry. Controlled, but very angry.

"It's easy for you to sit back and criticise." Her eyes flashed at me. "What about taking responsibility for your own part in the system?"

I was taken totally off-guard. Wow, was she being defensive!

I left churned up inside. Her criticisms nagged away in the back of my mind over the next few days. I thought of a million rejoinders, all eloquent and many cutting. I went to sleep turning over the twists in communication that had sneaked into our review process.

And turning over my motives. My desire had been to encourage all along the way. I was baffled that my friends couldn't clearly see it!

So I sat at my plate of wedding fare with a heavy heart and watched my friend. Had she acknowledged to herself how hurtful her comments had been? Then a worrying thought intruded - is it me who's being defensive now? It had all become so confused. I meant well. At least I thought I did.

God is sovereign and I must trust him to assess correctly and sort us out. Isn't he the true judge?

Misunderstanding is fertile soil for criticisms and accusations. When attacked, most beings will defend. One way or another.

Nowhere is that clearer than at home with the children. One son comes crying into the kitchen, complaining that the other has thrown him against the couch. The accused follows, loudly justifying himself. "Oh sure, you're always getting hurt and of course you never do anything. Mum, he was pushing me over and over even when I told him to stop. I just pushed back and he went into the couch. I didn't mean to. But you never believe me. You always accept what he says."

The recurring ability of each of my children to sincerely fulfil the role of an injured innocent party is nothing short of amazing. We grown-ups are the same. We're simply more sophisticated about it. God has had longer to work on us, too, so hopefully we're somewhat more detached from our self-justification.

Exactly what is it we need to defend so ferociously? Do we need to be right to be worthwhile as people? Do we need to maintain a particular image of ourselves?

When you boil it down, the gospel says we are justified by Jesus and have complete security in him. He is our shield and protector. He is our lover, counsellor and friend. When we jump to defend and justify ourselves out of inner insecurity we forget who we are. We move out of his embrace.

So the first step in moving through defensiveness is remembering our security in Jesus. It's all right to explain ourselves and present truth as we see it. But if we need to be right, if communication flows from an inner frenzy of self-protection, we will find attacks at many turns and become experts at defence.

When we let go of the need to be right, we step over a threshold. We can begin to engage with issues, with the actual content of feedback. This is the second step in moving through defensiveness. When life throws you criticism, set aside the feelings. Give them to Jesus. It might take time. Then sift through the actual content of what is being said. Respond to that.

When I can receive feedback about myself with the same openness I would bring to a frank discussion about someone else, when I put aside instinctive defence in response to being attacked, I've found the gate in the fence. I've moved out into a whole new open world.

ENTERTAINING ANGELS

❦

"*E*veryone should have a Belgian house guest. They're incredibly helpful. I thoroughly recommend it." My friend's smiling face appeared at my door. She was reflecting on her current guest, a man her son had met on his travels in Europe. Addresses had been swapped and invitations issued. Mike was one traveller who took up the invitation. This friend's open house is amazing. Mike was one of many who have shared their family life over the years.

Such families amaze me. Do you know women who keep producing meals and making people welcome? The extra dishes, the extra sheets on the line, the interruption to work and routine—none of that seems to matter. My family and friendship circle includes people exceptionally gifted that way. Long before we called hospitality an industry it was a way of life for these people. Christmas celebrations and camping holidays include guests. It may be an overseas traveller passing through like Mike. Maybe a longer-term addition to the family. The range has been diverse and all have been welcome: English women teaching their way around Australia, returned missionaries, single mums, children's friends and their parents, sailors in port for a few days and troubled teenagers for a few years.

It's beautiful to be made welcome. I enjoy being included, feeling as if someone is relaxed with me around. The gospel is God's heart of hospitality. He has done what is necessary to include me. He can relax with me. I am welcome.

For a season of my life I had other people in our home most of the time. Even if I did not succeed in making people truly welcome there was a lot of contact. Life isn't like that now and I'm glad. It was too much. For my friend, the people contact never seems too much. She doesn't get peopled out like me. Wisdom lies in knowing yourself. If I try to copy my friend I'll fall flat on my face. I operate differently inside. However, God expects me to reflect him and he is hospitable. His life is open. Remember the veil in the temple that Friday?

My mother-in-law is gifted in hospitality and her welcome has resounded through the wider family over three generations now. Cousins and spouses travel hundreds of kilometres to join extended family holidays. The same gift is strong in the next generation. Like all gifts from God, hospitality compounds. It's like watching a great wave gather momentum.

Our sister and brother-in-law's extended family included a single mum for some years. Tragically she suicided last year, but her little boy will still come from interstate to share some holiday time. Who can see what God will do with that relationship in the long term?

A wedding this year brought a family of seven from the UK. to South Australia—another connection in a twenty-year friendship from travelling days. Hospitality allows relationships to form and grow. Relationships that span continents and generations. Relationships that are unpredictable and rich tools in God's hand.

In Hebrews 13:2 God said directly, "Do not forget to entertain strangers, for by so doing some people have entertained angels without knowing it." He doesn't want women to be kitchen-maids or drudges but he does want us to choose a lifestyle that has space in it for others and for the unexpected. In our culture that requires conscious thought—and it requires some measure of servant mentality in the home.

A big step for me was asking people back for toasted sandwiches or scrambled eggs. I keep a stack of frozen pizzas and pasties etc too. I'm not a woman who cooks for pleasure; since we all live with the stresses of affluent Western society, why not make use of some of the advantages?

Sometimes there have to be protected times—lines drawn across the calendar. I can't live without space for myself, my marriage and our family life. It's a battle to hang on to those basics. However, if we ask Jesus to move us in his direction each day he will unfold ways in which we can be welcoming, ways that work for us. Maybe one day I'll even have a Belgian house guest.

A HOUSE DIVIDED

"*S*ome nights I just go out into the backyard and pray to my heavenly Father. Loudly. I call on Jesus in the dark, under the stars." My friend's dark eyes gazed at me, troubled, and she broke into a self-conscious laugh. "Sometimes it's the only way to get through."

I often think of her calling out under the stars, or crying into the laundry tub in her cold lean-to. She raised her numerous children in days before they could afford a washing machine. By the time we became friends, she was 60. The children had grown and gone, but she still lived with her husband who didn't know Jesus. And she still had backyard vigils.

Her frustration was not new to me. My own mother lived with the same struggle and I grew up observing it from close range. Now women I love in my own generation tell me about the specific anguish that goes with being married to someone who doesn't share a love for Jesus. It is difficult, a painful reality to come to terms with.

My friend and my mother are hardworking women. Both have stubbornly persevered in serving God in the church in spite of opposition. Not every spouse in their position can manage that.

If you know Jesus, then you know his word says plainly not to marry a person who doesn't follow him. Paul warned solemnly about being "unequally yoked", invoking images of oxen unable to plow together effectively. However, faithfulness in marriage is a high value of God's. Hence the dilemma of those who find themselves pulling in different directions after the marriage is in place. So often spiritual inequality develops or emerges after marriage. If the partner consents to stay in the relationship, then there's no bailing out. That's clear from 1 Corinthians 7:12-16. God promises to provide all we need, and his promises must kick in here.

So how do you grow spiritually while living with someone who doesn't share your beliefs? The question applies not only to marriages but also to those living with siblings, parents or even children in a Christian family system that is not focused on Christ.

Firstly, in order to grow, spiritual life must be protected.

Modern Western life has much to offer spiritually, but it's far from being a rose garden. Sometimes it's more like a battlefield with poisonous gases wafting around. Every magazine stand and supermarket checkout exudes an atmosphere so superficial it can scarcely sustain breath. We can't buy a loaf of bread without seeing some subtle or overt image of human degradation. It's even harder to face at home, with a moral sewer running through our living rooms courtesy of the TV.

Whatever interests your family, whatever the level of cultural or intellectual activity, chances are that if you live with people who don't know Jesus your view of relaxation will be at odds with the household. It will be a constant stone in your soul's shoe. To protect your spiritual life you must be vigilant and dependent on God. Don't get drawn into movies or parties or drinking that will poison you. Remaining free yet gentle and gracious in relationships—that is the work of the Spirit in you. He will breathe real air from heaven into you if you let him.

Tension with your family is almost unavoidable. Certainly you will experience tension. However, this is fodder for growth if you accept it and actively submit it to God. Your family may react oversensitively to Jesus in you. Don't serve up a critical or self-righteous spirit for them to choke on.

Underneath, your family will know your attitude by the tone of your communication with them. You don't have to do everything they do to prove you love them or to keep the doors open, especially if what they are doing is wrong. Caring about them and being relaxed with them will be more powerful than going to the latest R-rated movie together. Of course, if you can find a good movie then enjoy it together.

A good sense of humour oils the wheels of any household. I wish I'd been better at fun when living at home in my youth. A word to wives here. It's quite OK with God to put creative effort into your sexual relationship with your husband. This can be a tricky area. With explicit material on just about anything readily available, you may have to draw boundaries and protect them. Along with that, though, some humour and some wholehearted involvement in your relationship with your husband can go a long way.

The second pitfall to avoid is believing the lie: What's God got to do with real life? The church is for the weak and old women. Satan sees to it that a powerful message about the foolishness, irrelevance and hypocrisy of faith oozes out everywhere and especially hits you when you go home. Take this assault seriously and be vigilant with protective prayer. Is there a special friend who can be prayer partner in this?

Don't let Satan suck you dry of vitality with his insidious lies. God is the great, and ultimately the only reality. You're on the winning side. Sneak a look at the end of the book and you'll see.

So far I've mentioned only pitfalls and protective measures. What about growing?

My dark-eyed friend prays under the stars at night. A new friend, Ann, also in her 60s, lived for many years in a spiritually unequal marriage. She told me that she would get up very early in the morning to pray.

"In the hard times I grew so much closer to the Lord."

When Ann started to awaken as a Christian, she was many years into her marriage with children aged 13, 15 and 18. She began going to church and talking a lot about Jesus at home. "That got on my husband's nerves. I wasn't so careful back then."

Over the years Ann learnt a different way. "After a while I didn't talk about faith much at home and I certainly didn't argue with the family about it. I had friends pray a great deal for me and my family."

To grow, everyone needs relationships with others in Jesus, to study the Bible and to serve and give in some way. Ann found ways to do all that without pushing it at her family.

"Later in my walk with Jesus I became involved in parachurch activities. I was able to study the Bible and pray with friends during the week. Then there was a season of ministry with a women's outreach organisation which was wonderful and didn't require weekend time. I found the key was not allowing my Christian involvements to interfere with the family. I kept my activities to my own time. That meant no phone calls in the evenings and other times when the family was home. All the women involved in the ministry respected that. We prayed for each other's families."

Ann was once asked to be involved in a Billy Graham crusade but felt it wouldn't work and so didn't even ask her husband about it. Then, on the relevant weekend her husband went on a fishing trip with a relative unexpectedly and she could attend the crusade. He had never been on a fishing trip before. God gives gifts like that.

There are wonderful opportunities for women to both study the Bible and exercise ministry gifts through parachurch groups. Movements like Know Your Bible (KYB) and Bible Study Fellowship (BSF) bring life to thousands of women in Australia.

Many churches have Bible study groups and service opportunities during the week too. God will direct you to a fruitful place if you ask him and keep your eyes open.

Being part of a church where people really love Jesus is great, of course. If your family can live with that, then go for it. My mother took that course and it was very important to her to do so. Every step was a battle. There wasn't much available to her during the week in the 1960s in our area. But there's a lot available now.

As a daughter in the household I enjoyed freedom to go to church and youth activities which were life to me. I never tried to preach in any way at home and kept up with household chores and my school work. That way if Dad challenged me he had no grounds for complaint. I believe our years of silence allowed my mother and me to speak directly in the crucial final weeks of Dad's life when God broke through his defences.

Close relationship is vital. And Bible study and prayer. We are not made to walk out the faith in a broken world alone. This is equally relevant if your family believes but isn't pursuing Jesus as you want to. Just yesterday a friend mentioned that she is grateful her husband is a believer but struggles with the fact that going to church regularly is not a priority for him.

"It wears me down", she said. That's it. Fanning the flame in your own spirit while living in a house divided wears you down.

That's why it's vital to find points of connection to the Lord, to his word and to his people. Connections that will disrupt your family as little as possible.

But the starting point is acceptance of your lot. How true that always seems to be. It is hard to live with people antagonistic to or threatened by your faith. Don't underestimate the challenge.

And don't undervalue your faithfulness under difficulty. Comparing yourself to others in different families will only set you up for misery. You can't be in every ministry you want if your husband is opposing you at home. Standing firm in Jesus when the ground around your feet is eroding each day—this gives the angels joy. Loving those God has given you to love and serve, embracing the limitations—this is valued in eternity. God's purpose is to display who he is by his nature in us. He can do that powerfully in our family relationships as well as in our activities in the world.

We each have our own race to run. We each need God's grace to do it. And we each receive a crown when we arrive home. We don't all set off from the same starting block but we end up at the same table.

FAMILY DEVOTIONS IN THE 21ST CENTURY?

"*I*t's unbelievable. Those people just didn't get it! So thick," burst Melanie. She was exasperated by the stream of idol-worshipping kings in Judah and Israel. First and Second Kings do make frustrating reading. We threw around some thoughts on how we can be the same and the children drifted off, either to do homework or to hassle each other 'for fun'.

Eighteen months ago we decided to read through the Bible as a family before the children start leaving home. It's a long project but it feels right. We'll pack them off into the world with at least one complete exposure to God's word, apart from Sunday school etc.

During primary school, children respond to one-on-one devotional times at bedtime. Christian bookshops supply a range of suitable materials. Sometimes the desire extends into high school, which is great.

It doesn't take long to go through a short reading, devotional thought or activity and a prayer. In our house the privilege has belonged to Dad. At this point two of the children still want it—a precious opportunity. With the older children we settle for a short one-on-one prayer time before bed most days.

There are materials for guided family devotions out there, too. In the children's early years (up to age ten or 11) books with short devotional readings were very successful. In later years we have occasionally found them useful—mainly at Christmas time. Generally, though, we haven't had as much success with books as the children grew older.

Following a guided reading program with questions, activities and prayers can be wonderful, especially with younger children. Such a habit needs to be cultivated early. Children won't behave like sedate adults and hence the crucial importance of a simple activity. Once the children can read, horizons expand. They love to take turns reading a Bible verse or prayer.

Our own experience has been patchy, and at times I've felt uneasy and inadequate about the whole thing. As a Christian family we should have been praying together more. If I close my eyes and imagine family devotions I see attentive children respectfully listening to the Bible. I see genuine discussion of the meaning of the passage. Of course the children never argue. In fact, they're struck by their own failings and want to be soft and kind towards their siblings. The shiny-faced cherubs eagerly pray for each other, all the while bathed in a golden haze of light.

With my eyes open, that's not what I see. In fact, romantic images of family devotions are a great enemy to getting started at all. So after years of patchiness we embarked on the reading project. Our children were old enough by then—all over ten. We decided to simply let God's word speak.

We didn't think we'd manage a specific, separate time for Bible reading. It's hard enough to find time together as a family at all. However, most nights we do eat dinner together. In itself that is a great strength. So we added in a chapter of the Bible, inserting some New Testament when the Old Testament laws and history need a little rest. After main course I serve dessert and Allan reads. That way the children are occupied eating for some of the time. The children get restless sometimes; they interrupt and can be plain silly. It's basic but we're doing it.

We often have discussion about the content. Sometimes we share what is happening, or has happened, in our relationship with God. Occasionally we pray around the table and more occasionally we have communion together. As parents we try to avoid being know-it-alls. We share our understanding of difficult passages and leave it at that. When we don't understand a passage we say so. Sometimes we've finished by lying on the living room floor listening to a song on a CD.

We're sure God is at work in our weakness. He promised his word would never return to him empty. When a child is baptised, or christened, or dedicated, the parents promise to raise that child in the knowledge of God. The unique honour of sharing God's word with our children in our home belongs to us. We are their parents and our time with them is really very short.

No two families are the same and your way of doing devotions will end up different from everyone else's. God is with you, though. He is for you. If you're doing it, hang in there. If you're not, make a beginning.

OUR FAMILY CHRISTMAS COULD
USE SOME PRAYER

❦

*I*n real life pain and pleasure often go hand in hand. Christmas celebrations are no exception.

For many of us, Christmas is a positive part of our culture and childhood memories. When we were growing up, Christmas meant the end of school, the anticipation of presents, a buzz in the household, the smell of good food, friends and relatives getting together —it was a highlight of the year. Now, as grown women, much of the delight is in giving rather than receiving. Isn't it fun wrapping presents for children or anyone you love, imagining their delight? Isn't it wonderful getting together with people you love? And who doesn't enjoy the feasting?

At the same time, though, Christmas in Australia coincides with end of school year activities and so most parents and teachers are doubly tired. We have to try to simplify Christmas preparation out of necessity. The frenzied present buying, cooking and card writing of December all compromise the pleasure of the day for many women. We're exhausted.

And that's not all. Around the world, those who love Jesus grieve and strain over the way he gets pushed aside at Christmas time, in spite of the fact that Christmas bears his name. In our country it's the same. One of the central joys of Christmas is the special music and worship, the wonder of Jesus' coming. Yet Aussies on the whole scarcely give Jesus a mention. Christmas has come to be about presents, food, holidays and 'rellie bashes'.

It feels strange to bask in the special celebrations at church while friends and neighbours go through what seem to us empty motions. We rightly put effort into helping and challenging each other to keep the focus on Jesus. If we don't use Christmas to enjoy Jesus' presence in worship and to share his love with people around us, it feels shallow.

However, the focus of my thoughts leading up to December this year is that central institution of Christmas: the rellie bash. It's a source of so much joy for some, and so much grief for others. When everyone is supposed to be having a wonderful get-together, laughing, singing and expressing love through giving gifts, how miserable to be alone or in conflict with family members. How many Christmas get-togethers are trials, borne with gritted teeth and oiled with beer? How many degenerate into argument or hurt feelings hidden behind polite facades?

God has given me a lovely gift in the past two years. He prompted two other members of my extended family and me to pray. We have each prayed for the family individually, of course. Now we actually get together to do it. I feel at last that I'm doing something productive for my siblings and in-laws and nieces and nephews. We believe God has been at work in our family during that period. The annual Christmas get-together gives an opportunity to appreciate that. This year, with another year of agreeing in prayer and asking in Jesus' name under our belts, we're expecting to see further evidence of his work.

If your family get-together at Christmas yields more pain than pleasure or highlights the challenges of being family, don't accept that nothing can ever change. Prayer is more powerful than we realise, even when we pray believing. Join with a like-minded partner to pray for your family; that might be better than any gift you can give them.

I plan to continue preparing for Christmas all year by praying for my family. Bring on the rellie bash! Jesus is invited, and he's such a wonderful and surprising guest.

PARENTING: A BRIEF LABOUR FOR A LIFETIME'S IMPACT

THE WINDOW

(FOR GEORGINA)

Was the sky ever before so blue?
Sheer solid unadulterated blue.
Has a gull's cry ever rung so pure?
A caw dropped from his throat
into the measureless cavern of the sky;
raw, crude, reverberating to the edge
of my otherwise silent world.

How warm and soft the sun feels on my arm
through a small, diamond-glassed window.

High in this stone house
I fling open the tiny window
and see God's whole big world.
I see it and feel it
from the safety of a stone attic.

Perhaps this stone house has stood,
not for hundreds of years,
but forever.
Perhaps this day never dawned,
but always was.

Perhaps I'll never move.
Perhaps there's nothing more or other than
this deep, warm quiet.

But no.
This morning Henry was born.
Of course he already existed in your mind, Lord,
and in the secret darkness of my womb.

But this morning he left my body
and entered the world.
He lives now,
not only in your mind,
and in secret.
He lives before our eyes.
We have had a beginning.

I am exhausted at this point
of end and beginning.
I have laboured
and now I am at rest.
I give him back to you already.
I give myself back to you.

Let us always live before your face.
Let this deep, warm silence of eternity
always lie in my heart.
I lay myself down in you.

BALANCING ACT

*B*rowsing for greeting cards recently I spotted such a cute one. It was one of those unlikely animal cards: a cat riding a unicycle holding a horizontal pole in front. Perched on each end of the pole was a small mouse, and another creature sat on the cat's head. Quite a feat! I bought it for a friend who felt at the time as if she was going to fall off her bike.

Since then the picture has often popped into my mind. Who doesn't sometimes feel like that cat, straining every muscle, wobbling around and about to lose it all?

For a woman who works as a Family Administrator (my husband's term and I like it), the job specification includes plenty of balancing acts. If more than one child lives in the house, balancing the demands and interests of each with the others is inevitable. One goes off in a huff feeling neglected because she asked you to come and you haven't. The reason for the delay was another child who called you to look at a rash on a private part of her anatomy and you got talking about some personal things. Taking the opportunity seemed important.

The second child also started out frustrated because she waited for quite a while with her rash ready and her bedroom door closed. You were held up by a squabble between two children and the need to kill a big black spider in the toilet for one of them. Big black spiders won't wait.

This kind of situation is the daily stuff of life. With the time pressures on us all it's a battle to create and guard family time.

Then there's the balancing of husband time with time as a family. Marriages thrive on care and attention, just like the families that spring from them. Exciting as it is to work together as partners in raising children and other pursuits, we need to focus on ourselves as couples, too. Many an evening Allan and I say in a whisper, "Let's go up to our room early tonight and hang out." Unfortunately, life usually interferes with such intentions. But we do try.

With older children going to bed later than we want to, time together as a couple generally costs us time with the children. It feels weird and isn't easy to pull off. Sometimes it's simpler to arrange a weekend away. Marriage won't thrive only on that, though. The daily and weekly round needs to include time focused on each other. I guess that's why husbands and wives sleep in the same bed.

Even then, it's possible to go to sleep and wake up quite separately. Apparently most couples actually sleep the night with their backs to each other. We do. A simple investment in your husband is to face him in bed and touch him in some way to say goodnight and to greet him in the morning. It's a conscious choice.

Individual activities pull away at cohesive time. Phone calls, visitors, relationships with the wider world all impinge. This is another of our balancing acts.

Families must relate beyond themselves. We are members of wider blood families and church families. We are part of neighbourhoods and citizens of communities. We live in a big, exciting, overwhelming and complex world. God wants us as whole families and each individually to be present in our world. He is present in us.

However, a 21st century danger is that we will lose a cohesive sense of family belonging. We can be spread too thin. A sense of family is foundational to identity. We parents must guard some space for our families apart from the complex dynamic wider world.

We try to have some nights in the week free from visitors and outside commitments. We never watch TV while eating dinner and we usually read the Bible together when it's just our family at the table. We have an answering machine and screen most calls, never answering during dinner. Sometimes I declare a moratorium on social life for an afternoon or a day, including an occasional day in the school holidays.

God will give us a way through the delicate maze if we ask him. We need to listen to him, to our families and to our hearts.

Whether the pole we're trying to carry while riding our bike has two children on the ends or marriage time balanced with family time or wider relationships, God can and will keep us upright and pedalling. Family was his idea.

LETTING GO

❧

entle brown eyes filling up over steaming coffee. Kate was struggling today.

"I feel so helpless. If I had my choice, I would never send such a young child away from me for so long. But I just couldn't manage the home schooling any more." A tear trickled down one cheek.

"God gave us this child to raise and now I send her off to some teacher who doesn't know us at all. I don't have any idea what's happening to my own daughter all those hours."

Kate's oldest child started school this morning. She is seven and has gone into Year 2. After two years of home schooling Kate found herself unable to continue. Her third child was born a few months ago and needs a lot of attention with recurring croup. Sleepless nights and an active toddler have left Kate wasted. She couldn't give home schooling her best shot any more.

But it is so hard to let go. It is so hard to entrust a precious child to a stranger, to the education machine.

Casting my mind back, I pictured my oldest child's first day at school. I had a three-year-old and a one-year-old and was six months pregnant at the time. It was a momentous feeling of vulnerability handing my treasure over. I was flat out, though, and didn't have space to dwell too much on the child who was the big one in the system. I couldn't consider home schooling as an option. It would have been beyond me.

We have sent our children to public schools so far, feeling called to be present in the local school community. So over the years we have seen each child off into the hands of whatever teacher they happened to get.

I told Kate about God's assurances that he watches the children. One year we felt distinctly uneasy about our second child's teacher. It was nothing we could put our finger on. We prayed, and soon after received a phone call asking if we'd mind her being shifted to another class. She could choose a friend to take with her if she and the parents liked! The school, of course, thought they were acting on unexpected enrolments. We knew God was at work.

It's possible to be part of the classroom routine these days, by helping out each week. It's a great opportunity to get a feel for what's happening in your child's life at school. I remind myself regularly that our children are not our own. They belong to their Father God and he loves them far more than we do.

When we pray and come to conviction about God's plan for a child we have to confidently release that child to him. We cannot be with our children everywhere. They are lent to us for a while but they belong to God. He will always go with them. And he knows we're not perfect.

Our current struggle is letting go at another step along the process. Our oldest is in his final year at school. We have to let him find his own way in study and time priorities. It's amazingly hard. We're stretching and straining inside, finding great difficulty standing back and watching the choices he makes. We see major stress for him as the year unfolds, and underachievement and limited options for his future. He sees uptight parents who baffle him with their seriousness and frustrate him with their reactions.

When I'm praying about him I'm quite clear. I feel at peace about a hands-off approach. And underneath I'm optimistic because our son is in God's hands. He will learn and respond to life's realities. But not if we don't let him go.

Then he makes another choice to procrastinate and socialise and all my anxieties spring up. It's an emotional habit that comes from my sense of inadequacy, not from faith in God: I've failed to train and shape him properly. And I fear the consequences for him.

This is a growth point for my spirit now. I will listen to God and not be howled down by my fears and inadequacies. I have to let my son go in this area; he doesn't go into a vacuum. But there are no guarantees, either.

From the momentous exit of a baby from my body to the momentous exit of an adult child from my home, loving involves letting go. The one who was within me, then always with me, and now sometimes with me, will soon move into a life separate from me.

At each step along the way we need God's grace. We love our children and cherish them. But we hold them lightly with God's arms always underneath.

SWEET OR SOUR?

SPEAKING POSITIVELY TO OUR CHILDREN

"*S*ticks and stone may break my bones, but words will never hurt me." We sang that in the schoolyard, but it isn't true. Words have power to hurt. They also have power to build.

Studies of modern families indicate an alarming lack of interaction between parents and children. Some studies report only three or four minute conversations per day between a given pair. That's hard to believe. If you exchange but few words in a day, they need to count. However, regardless of the length of time you talk with your child, it's important what you say. Your words build part of the foundation of your children's self-concept and understanding of the world.

Some years ago I remember a rare experience of travelling for several hours on a train. I was going to visit my sister and I relished the opportunity to sit quietly with my newest baby. I could focus on her, leaving the other three at home with Dad. As she nodded off to the bumpity-bump of the train, my attention was caught by a woman travelling with three primary-school-aged children. They seemed a tight-knit family, the children chatting together cheerfully. I was particularly struck by the bright, positive way the mother spoke to her children. My heart warmed to the fuzzy sentiments tumbling in me about mothering and families.

The mother bought drinks and chips, producing smiles all

round. Then the predictable happened. Someone spilt their drink, and sticky Fanta sloshed from the seat to the floor.

What a transformation! Mother's face and body hardened. She got stuck into the children with no apparent awareness of anyone else in the carriage. "You stupid @#%*$ idiots! You're always so clumsy. How many times have I told you to be careful? But do you listen? Do you ever take any notice? No, of course not. Well, that's the last time I buy anything on this trip."

And so it went. The children stiffened immediately and sat like little, stunned jack rabbits. They looked completely miserable and didn't utter a word. I'm not even sure they breathed for a minute or two.

The contrast in that woman's behaviour was shocking. In a minute I moved from secret admiration to miserable pity for those poor kids. It was only some Fanta, after all, only childish irresponsibility, not genuine defiance. Yet her words left them in no doubt of their status as disobedient, worthless, clumsy kids.

Perhaps it was an especially bad day. Getting up early to make a train is never easy with children. But I couldn't help imagining those children hearing hostile messages over and over. What hurt and resentment would that build in their hearts? My resolve to speak positively to my children was renewed. How often it has had to be renewed since!

We can give positive words spontaneously, and we can learn to deliver negative content in more positive ways. We can also order the family system in a way that will facilitate positive interactions, rather than making them harder.

A gift of love

Firstly, to initiate kind talk is to give a gift of love. Each day affords its chances. Have you seen light spread over your child's face in response to an unexpected word of appreciation? It's like the sunrise. So, rather than taking your children's strengths for granted, how about praising them?

"You were very organised this morning. Well done."

"That was kind to let Mary play with your bucket."

Sure, it is Johnny's job this week to do the dishes, but life is easier for you when he does. It doesn't take long to say, "Thank you for doing those dishes, Johnny. You are getting quicker, I think, and I appreciate them being done." Or "How about a hug? Mothers need hugs from their children, you know?" Even the basic "I love you" All these words are gifts to your children. Unappreciated for now, perhaps, but messages of love and respect will filter into their souls.

Basic courtesy is part of initiating positive talk. No matter how young the child, he or she should be asked to do a task with a "Please" and thanked afterwards. She or he should be looked at when spoken to and not yelled at from another room. And it is hypocritical to ask a child to do something if you are actually issuing an order. Still, even orders can be delivered in positive, respectful ways.

Positive correction

Life is not all praise, hugs and strengths, of course. It's also provocation, strain, frustration, instruction and correction. When your little darling snaps at you for the third time in a morning, something has to be done. There is a choice of response though.

"How dare you speak to me like that? I have had quite enough of you and your bad temper. You will not be having Rebecca to play today, and I'll tell her why too, you rude girl." A better, more positive response is "That is completely inappropriate behaviour, and I will not tolerate you speaking to me like that. I expect an apology please."

Your dreamer is still sitting among his toys and knick-knacks after being asked more than once to pack up and bring his lunch box to the kitchen. Music practice, setting the table and homework still lie ahead, and he manages a grunt at best when you call his name. Your patience is wearing thin. Again you have a choice of response.

"Why do I waste my breath? You don't listen to a single thing I say, do you? You just ignore me, and it's beyond me why I even bother. But of course, good old Mum will always do her part. Good old Mum will make sure every thing is OK. Anyone would think I was your slave!"

The cost of letting off steam like that is hurt and resentment in your child. He gets the message that you feel exploited and think little of him as a person. By all means communicate what you feel but let it be with respect. Make clear eye contact and keep your voice as normal as possible.

"I feel so frustrated when I ask you multiple times to start your jobs and you show no sign of doing it. Don't you hear me? I don't want to believe that you don't care about me, but that's the message I could get from your behaviour." Not caring is far from your child's mind at that point. This scenario leads straight into the matter of setting up a helpful family system.

A helpful structure

Few children are automatically organised, self-motivated and able to anticipate what needs to be done around the home. Most don't even know what you mean by "Put your clothes away, please". The burden of teaching these basic skills, as well as the more complex areas of life and relationships, can weigh heavy. And many mothers feel this burden as an emotional pressure. It's easy then to take the children's non-compliance personally. And that is a great enemy of positive communication.

In order to function under the burden of training children, we need to shift a lot of the day-to-day weight from our shoulders to an external system. There is power and freedom in a set of negotiated rules with clearly stated consequences. Parents must lay the ground rules, make the expectations clear and follow through with the consequences. That sounds easy. In real life it takes commitment, but it's much easier on everyone in the long run.

In our house, the most effective consequence at the moment is loss of access to the Nintendo N64. The children's turns are allocated to particular days and times, but their chart of tasks for the previous day has to be up to date. We still use time out in bedrooms too, though not as much as when the children were younger.

The power of a functional system to relieve emotional pressure was driven home again recently. My husband was away, and I found myself entangled nearly every day in wearing interactions. Making sure jobs were done and music practised, discouraging the children from rough-housing and getting bodies up and organised in the morning in good time seemed an unattainable ideal. I went to bed most nights feeling defeated by the frustrated and negative tone of my interactions with the children. Such patches are demoralising.

Then I realised I'd forgotten the rule, "No N64 if your chart for the day before is not completed". The light went on in my head. And after recovering from this temporary amnesia, I found life straightforward. I put a little energy into reminding everyone of the system, then let the rules do the work. "It's time for your turn? Well, did you get everything done yesterday? No? Oh, well. I'm sorry, but no N64 today."

The relief was glorious. With an 'objective' system to carry much of the load, I was freed of the cycle of frustration and defeat. I had space to speak positively and kindly to my children. So once again I learnt that I need actions to provide the structure for positive words. Our family needs a system to facilitate kindness.

What a great task God gives us in giving us children. If we want them to grow and flourish with dignity, and we want to walk in joy and dignity ourselves, we must master our tongues. We have power to do great good or harm with what comes out of our mouths. Let's speak words of life into the lives of our children.

TAMING THE BEAST IN THE LIVING ROOM

*The TV's in the cellar again", Jane smiled. She occasionally puts their TV away for a while. Another family doesn't own one at all. I was always impressed with the creativity of their sons who built and made rather than watched.

Karl Marx said that religion was the opiate of the people. He hadn't seen TV.

In our home we have never put the TV away. A lot of energy has gone into controlling it, though.

During pre-school years the children watched Play School and the short children's programs following on the ABC. Phones ran hot between mothers at 4:30 pm! I was alarmed, though, to discover households where the TV was always on. Friends at play group worried about getting their children to pre-school on time. I was baffled until they mentioned that the children turned on cartoons first thing. Our children didn't turn the TV on without permission.

School years are a different ball game. Early in that season for us, our pastor suggested a one week moratorium on TV watching. Many church families took it up. Our children were resistant but eventually willing to try it. The week was surprisingly easy and pleasant. I believe it broke something. At the end, I suggested we could live without TV during the week. To my surprise, the children

137

agreed. We consciously resolved to limit the TV to weekends. So for ten years we have watched TV only on weekends, mainly videos. Videos are great. No ads, and you have control.

Now, in the season of high school and university, things are changing again. Last year we made one weeknight concession and watched Smallville with the kids. Our oldest son, at 18 years, is now free to make his own choices, but house rules still apply at home.

Here are a few guidelines that have helped keep us on track:

- Watching is planned, not impulsive.
- If watching a commercial station, mute the ads. It robs them of power. (This worked best when the children were in primary school.)
- No channel surfing.
- No watching TV before church on Sunday.

Even now, the children do not have TVs in their bedrooms. This keeps viewing out in the open and requires communication. Recently we put a second set in the master bedroom. Now a subset of the family can snuggle with a favourite movie, but only with parents' permission. Our main set is in the family room, which is a thoroughfare. We're blessed with a separate living room which is strictly TV free.

Around these simple guidelines flow many hours of debate and discussion about suitable movies. It's a big issue in our family life and one we believe merits energy and attention.

I was surprised and delighted recently to overhear my 15-year-old talking about TV in the car with his friends. "I used to get so mad with my parents when I was younger because they wouldn't let us watch much TV. I thought they were so strict. Now I'm really glad, because I think it's such a waste of time."

The comment was not directed at me. I would never have known he thought that way if I hadn't been the chauffeur that day. Of course, since he's a teenager, his views are subject to change without notice. But it was a great encouragement, and felt like a little gift from the Lord on the day.

The TV is an incredible tool of communication that must be prayerfully controlled. A Jewish rabbi commented that a TV was like a moral sewer running through your living room. We have a responsibility to filter the flow and I ask God regularly for courage and vigilance to stick to the task.

ON BEING A YES-WOMAN

"*I*'ve told you about Ricky the rat, haven't I?"

Jenny's eyes danced as she leaned over to talk with me. She waved her arm in the direction of her son carrying Ricky on his arm.

"I blame it on Anne. She told me to say 'Yes' whenever I could."

By following Anne's advice Jenny had found herself mother not only to three children but also to one handsome grey and white rat. She, like me, called him beautiful from a distance but preferred not to touch him.

Last week I had a lovely experience saying 'Yes'. Melanie asked if she could bake some 'melting moments'. I felt like saying 'No'. It seemed like unnecessary mess and bother in a busy day. After a deep breath I remembered Anne's advice and said 'Yes, why not?' So an hour later I found myself sitting outside with a cup of tea and a melting moment served by my daughter. I really would have missed out by saying 'No'.

In the toss and tumble of daily mothering it's easy to say 'Yes' when we should stand firm on 'No', and to say 'No' when we could bend to 'Yes'.

In the first case, the system of boundaries and consequences should generally stay intact. Every day there is pressure from children to erode the system. They nag and whine and nibble away at the edges until we give in. But it's a mistake to do so. In the long run life will run much more smoothly if the rules and consequences remain in place. Music practice and homework should be done before watching TV or video games, if that's the agreed rule. Defiance should lead to time out and not be ignored. If it's an issue of undermining our authority and consistency we must maintain 'No'.

On the other hand, we're so easily inclined to react with 'No' to a request unrelated to rules, simply because it's an effort. Finger painting or chalk drawing on the back cement are so much fun. Sure, it takes time to clean up the kitchen after cooking melting moments, but what happy memories for the budding cook! Planting flowers or ironing the towels takes longer with a little off-sider but the extra time is an investment in the off-sider.

Last weekend our youngest had a friend for a sleepover. Much of Friday evening was spent in the bedroom building a fantastic fort from dining chairs, pegs, sheets and rugs. Both girls slept all night under the canopy they'd made. I had to crawl in amongst the teddies like a guerrilla fighter to snatch a kiss goodnight.

By Sunday I was locked in dispute with our daughter, wanting her to pack it up by Monday morning.

"Why?"

"We need to be organised and ready for the start of a new week."

This line of argument failed to impress her. Sunday got busy. I was worn down and couldn't be bothered. In the end the fort stayed. By Tuesday the pegs gave way and the sheet fell gently onto a sleeping girl. She collected the pieces and tidied her room. As I look back I wonder why it mattered to me. There was no harm in leaving the fort. It was no big deal to sit on folding chairs at the dining table for a couple of extra meals. I regretted creating an unnecessary issue. I could easily have said 'Yes' in the first place.

By establishing and maintaining a consistent system of rules we teach character and responsibility. It's hard but important work. Children who live with such consistency gradually learn discipline and respect. They learn to function effectively in the world. On the other hand, when it comes to optional extras, parents who say 'Yes' make life fun. A child whose parents make an effort and bend feels as if those parents are for him, not against him. This positive atmosphere oils the wheels of family life.

A 'Yes' that should have been 'No' (giving in) leads to heaviness and defeat. Not so with a 'Yes' that reaches out to make life fun. That turns a black-and-white day into living colour. I just hope my children don't ask me for a rat.

"MUMMY, WHY DID THEY DO THAT?"

❦

HELPING CHILDREN COPE WITH EVIL IN THE WORLD

*E*arly on the morning after September 11 2001, I was driving my teenage son on his newspaper round. Our TV hadn't been on the night before, so we had gone to bed blissfully unaware that the world had changed, devastated by the events in New York and Washington. The car radio finally alerted us, and we joined millions of other Westerners in a daze of shock and disbelief.

As the drama developed, with most of the city glued to TV sets, many churches in our area arranged calls to prayer. Our family joined a prayer meeting at our church, and the prayers certainly flowed. I was particularly struck by the response of children. Almost one-third of those present were children or teenagers, and several prayed at length and with feeling. That isn't usually the case at our general church prayer meetings.

Children were deeply affected by September 11, but they face sudden shock and loss at other times, too. They need us to help them learn to deal with these realities. Of course, they live in the same sin-polluted, distorted world that we do, and we must be their shelter and guide as much as we can. God shelters and guides us all, and we need his grace in us and through us to our children at such times.

Young children

Pre-school children will be quite confused by events like the

September 11 attacks. They have no concept of where the attacks are in relation to them and they have difficulty understanding that images of planes in the US are real events, not stories on TV. Young children will, however, be sensitive to the feelings of adults around them. They pick up the emotional tone. We mustn't panic.

Hugging is important in a time of shock. This won't just help the young child, but the adult, too!

Primary-age children

School-age children will want to know more about the events. It's helpful to look at maps and figure out just where world events are taking place. You can help by being open about your own feelings, but not overdoing it. They don't need to be overwhelmed by your fear or anxiety. Try to explain as simply and clearly as you can what has actually happened and why, and what factors contributed to this situation.

Children benefit by actively expressing their thoughts and feelings. Words may not be the main way they do it. Pictures, letters, puppet plays or dramas might work better. It's also very beneficial to do something to help victims of a disaster. Children can write letters, collect aid items or prepare a display for the community.

Teenagers

Although they may act tough, teenagers are affected by disasters, too. They may look strong to save face with friends at school, but feel quite insecure. Young people are the ones who get sent off to war, after all.

Obviously, adolescents know more and have more resources to cope with something like September 11. They don't react like adults, though. They tend to see the world in black-and-white terms. It's important to find out information and discuss reasons for world events to make some sense of it together. Teenagers could research newspapers and magazines for the family and so take an active role in becoming informed. It was our 15-year-old who voraciously consumed information after September 11 and consistently raised related topics at the dinner table.

Their black-and-white tendency does make adolescents vulnerable to stereotyping. They may hasten to label good guys and bad guys. With this age-group adults can share more of their understanding of the complexities of issues. We must strongly encourage our teens not to allow hatred to fester in their attitudes. Meeting some real-life Muslims in your area might be one way of defusing unhelpful stereotypes.

General approach

No matter what age children we are relating to, there are basic ingredients in the recipe for weathering world storms.

Open channels of communication

We need to keep listening, both to the words and to the non-verbal communication of our kids. Hugging helps. Sharing our own feelings in a controlled way helps. We don't have to have all the answers, but we must give the information we can and share our values as we interpret events. Right is right. Wrong is wrong. Our children want to know our convictions about the place of violence, the value of human life, and whether a military response is appropriate or not.

Build feelings of security

We can reassure children that most people are kind and don't want to hurt them. Remind children that many people in government and society generally are working very hard to keep them safe. Children in a country or suburban environment in Australia do not experience violent events as part of their everyday lives. Maintain the usual routines to reinforce the dependability and safety of their situation. Bath time, bed time, story time, school time, homework—let the daily round go on.

It's good to decrease images of violence in their lives. Turn off the TV if it's preoccupied with violent events. Commercial programming can be interrupted unexpectedly by frightening news bulletins. No useful purpose is served by stirring up nightmares and other fears and anxieties because of the media's desire to shock us and keep us watching.

Ask God for wisdom and search for understanding

Time is well spent purposefully searching out information that will help us and our children to understand. Seek out information without the vivid and frightening visual images. I found a couple of documentaries on the recent history of Afghanistan very helpful, for example. Most high-school-age kids would have understood them and would probably have found them genuinely useful in forming their views on September 11 and its aftermath. I'm less convinced about the value of endless images of planes flying into the World Trade Centre.

Most churches could easily find a missionary who has lived in a Muslim country, too. Maybe you and your children could initiate a visit from someone with an informed Christian understanding of Islam.

Pray

Paul wrote, "Don't fret or worry. Instead of worrying, pray. Let petitions and praises shape your worries into prayers, letting God know your concerns. Before you know it, a sense of God's wholeness, everything coming together for good, will come and settle you down. It's wonderful what happens when Christ displaces worry at the centre of your life" (Philippians 4:6-8, The Message).

We must remember that we are in a spiritual battle and God has much bigger purposes than we imagine. He has big purposes for nations as well as families and individuals. He is passionately concerned about our wellbeing, but our physical safety and comfort in this world are not the same thing as our wellbeing in eternal terms.

God is at work on the broad stage of world affairs. Nothing is outside of his control. Nothing shocks or surprises him. In fact he is working to bring his great redemptive good out of every circumstance. If we are to help our children grow into this vision, we must have it ourselves. If we are to help them trust him in spite of apparent disasters and all manner of perils, we must be at peace and trust him ourselves.

By praying with our children we strengthen our own trust as well as building theirs and modelling the very best approach to coping with tragedies, sorrows, griefs and disasters.

The following passages may be helpful to read together with your children, preferably in a modern version: Psalm 9:10, Psalm 55:22, 1 Peter 5:7, John 14:27, Psalm 27:1, Isaiah 54:14, Psalm 91:1,2, Psalm 32:7, 2 Thessalonians 3:3, Philippians 4:6-8.

TALKING POINTS

"Mum, look at that lady over there. Is she ever fat!"

"Why does that man walk so funny, Mum?"

Every parent of little children knows those moments when children pass comments about others in public ... and usually in loud voices. It can be very embarrassing. What is the best way to handle such situations?

The first instinct is to shut them up. No doubt you have seen a flustered parent grab her child's arm and yank hard. "For goodness' sake, Jessica, be quiet. Don't talk like that. It's rude." That is a possibility but not the recommended way to proceed. A young child will be confused by your angry reaction to straightforward observations. It's weird for them to be told off for speaking the truth. They need to understand what you are thinking. So what is a better way to respond?

Firstly, be discreet. Get your face close to your child's face and speak quietly.

Secondly, acknowledge what your child is saying. The person being observed probably is fat or is walking with an unusual gait. "Yes, she is large." Or "Yes, his way of walking is different from yours isn't it?"

Thirdly, give a clear but respectful message that the subject is closed for the moment. "Let's talk about it later." Then make sure you do talk about it later. Talk about how people feel.

You can discuss reasons why a person might be large. Perhaps she is pregnant or has a disease that makes her gain weight. Perhaps she is on medicine that has the same effect. The man might have been injured or have severe arthritis etc. Whatever the reason, it is important for the child to learn about people's feelings. "She is large but if she heard you commenting on it like that she might feel hurt. People feel sensitive about being looked at."

An example helps. Here is one I had to use a few years ago: "Remember when you started kindergarten in California and your accent was different from the other children? You were upset because Daniel kept calling out that you talked funny. I heard him yelling out at you to ask why you talked like that. It really hurt your feelings, didn't it?"

Curiosity is normal and to be encouraged. Sometimes you can pre-empt questions. If you see a situation that might arouse your child's curiosity it might be possible to approach the person in question. Make it a positive experience. "Would you mind telling my daughter about your cast?" or "... about your wheelchair?"

Children do not come with developed sensitivity to the feelings of others. We have to teach them but in a way they can receive. It's important not to shut them up or shut down their curiosity and openness.

This particular example of embarrassing public situations raises a more general matter of how we talk with our little children. I need to remind myself that my children do not belong to me, but to God. He made them, owns them and loves them more than I do. They are full human beings with the image of their maker in them and eternity before them, just like me. I must speak to them with respect. I have authority in their lives and must teach them respect for me. The parents are in charge.

However, even in exasperation I can speak respectfully. I can acknowledge them and what they say even when wanting to shape it and change it.

"She is large. Let's talk about it later" is different from "Don't talk like that!"

"I know you are mad at me but you have to go to your room now anyway", is different from "Don't you yell at me, young man!"

I cringe thinking about the times I have said things like "You kids never listen to me—what's the point of talking to you?" or "What is the matter with you—you're so selfish!" These are not exactly prime examples of respectful talk or effective training.

It's so wonderful to know I'm forgiven for my inadequacies and God is with me in parenting. Even in the severest warnings, he speaks respectfully to me. My prayer is for his grace to model that same way of talking to my children.

WHO'S CALLING THE SHOTS?

Not having been on a tram for years, I found the bumpity-bump comforting. My fixed gaze scarcely took in the backyards whizzing by, though. Why did it feel as if I was always fighting fires in mothering, always bouncing from disaster to demand? It makes a body feel like a slave after a while—a martyr even.

Leaving pressing chores to deliver the older children to a youth event, I had decided to take the younger ones on a mystery outing. I needed to initiate something positive. We would take a tram to the beach and buy an ice-cream. That would surprise the children and beat tidying bedrooms. They didn't seem excited, though, when the mystery was revealed. They wanted something different, like a trip to the movies. I had to exude quietly insistent cheerfulness as we sat at the tram stop. It would be fun in the end—but inside I felt demoralised.

Life and children press in on us. Every day could be packed with worthwhile activity, even if we planned nothing. We, as mothers, are structured to respond to our children's feelings and needs. By our responsiveness, they learn to trust, then flourish and find their way in the world. When children are tiny, we respond to their needs for safety, comfort, food and love. As they grow, their expression of those needs becomes more complex, and our response must change accordingly.

Children need to have an impact on their mothers. Their expressions of themselves and their initiatives need to make a difference. This affirms their expanding beings. Our children, however, are not in control of the family. God has delegated major authority to parents. This serves his purpose in more ways than we can currently grasp. We have the responsibility and privilege of leadership and so we set the tone. It's just that it doesn't always feel that way in the ebb and flow of the daily press.

As I sat glumly, I pondered the topic of initiative in my mothering. When the children were little, I needed to set clear rules and to strive to be consistent. That still applies as they get older but it becomes more subtle. More emotionally complex. I wasn't demoralised by a major failure in consistency. I just felt worn down by the waves of emotional demand and my feeling of chasing the action.

For some of us, built to respond instinctively to feeling, finding the balance between initiative and response takes some doing. Our children need to have an impact on us, but we set the tone. We need to have an impact on them, too.

Firstly, I need to stop. It's not often possible to withdraw for prayer, but I can pause on the inside. Quietness of spirit lets me register how I'm feeling and call to God in my heart. If I'm feeling pulled from place to place, I have to take stock. Otherwise I'll block the children (to control the pressure on me), and then they will get exasperated. In Ephesians 6:4a, Paul simply writes, "Fathers, do not exasperate your children". Some things never change.

Even though my calling as a mother is to serve, I don't have to be a slave to the desires of those around me. My goal is to relate proactively, not reactively, to my children. Not being naturally good at play, it would be a big step for me to suggest a game or cards after school. My natural approach is more to oversee the children as they relate to each other. But responding also requires initiative. How can I set the tone with my children this week? Notes in the lunch boxes, a simple game at my suggestion, sharing something I'm thinking about or planning in my own life, a little prayer before school as well as at bedtime, an offer to help with tidying the bedroom.

The tram ride wasn't a highlight of our week, but by the time we got home, a healthier balance had been restored. The children gradually warmed to the outing, and my sense of demoralisation dissipated.

Lord, save me from controlling and reacting. Give me grace to initiate and respond, for my children's sake and for my own.

PG KIDS IN AN R-RATED WORLD

*'m the only kid I know who has never seen an R-rated movie."

How many times have I heard that from our 14-year-old? What shall I say this time?

"So what?" (His chin sets grimly.)

"Aren't you fortunate?" (His eyes roll heavenward.)

"I find it hard to believe you're the only one." (He lists names.) Or:

"What R-rated movies do you want to see?" ("Nothing really, but ...")

So far our son makes noise but hasn't rejected our guidelines. We wonder what the next few years will bring.

Right now we are in the front line of instilling values in children. The challenge that countless generations have faced now faces us with all the particular flavours of postmodern Western culture. Surely every generation of children has complained of being hard done by and every generation of parents has been the strictest and the most unfair. So far we are in good company with our ancestors.

Never before, though, has there been a communication tool of the power and ubiquity of television. No generation has lived so much of its life before a silver screen, big or small, and thus been so generously immersed in the prevailing culture of the day. We don't give our children away to the lord of the manor or a religious order. No, they live with us. But the culture's values flow through our living rooms and bedrooms, invisibly filling the air. Our children's minds could be just as powerfully spirited away right under our noses.

We as parents feel undermined. We can't talk back to the silver screen. The gravelly bank is slipping away beneath our feet and we can't do a reality check with the TV character as we slide into the water.

However, we can and do have the most significant influence on our children. We can give them the gift of our values, in spite of the world around them.

Here are three keys to doing it: warmth, modelling and communication.

Warmth

What comes before the bond of parent and child? From the child's point of view, nothing. Children are born needing acceptance and affirmation. They are driven to extract these precious nectars from life, come what may. Through that need and vulnerability parents have a unique and powerful opportunity. Our children's receptor units are locked onto us and they will absorb our values by osmosis as we love, accept and affirm them.

Individuals express their needs differently and there are consistent differences between boys and girls.

In the 11 May 1998 edition of *Newsweek*, researchers reported what parents have known all along, that "boys will be boys". Generally they will not ask for attention in the way that girls do. However, boys need it just as their sisters do, even through the painful process of adolescent separation. As *Newsweek* said (p 58), "[During adolescence] parents have to try even harder to keep in touch. Boys want and need the attention but often just don't know how to ask for it." Girls don't know how to ask for it either. They might trail a parent arguing and venting feelings, seeming intractable. At least there is contact.

Whether expressing or withdrawing, every child and teenager needs love and affirmation. One of the highest levels of duty of all parents is commitment to giving this. A powerful tool is empathy, the validation of feeling. Even though you might want to leap straight into discussion and instruction with a child, pause a moment to reflect their feeling.

"I can understand that would be incredibly frustrating" doesn't take long to say but makes a huge difference to the quality of interaction.

The great bonus is this: as love successfully transmits into the being of a child, the values of the lover (parent) are smuggled in. It's a package deal. This is a basic dynamic of God's modus operandi. Reflect on your similarities as an adult to your own parents. Isn't the truth obvious? Remember the parting of ways with your parents in youth? Remember the humbling mid-life realisation that the ways seem to have re-converged? Life brings permutations. We are not replicas, but if you experienced your parents loving you, then chances are you hold their values deep down.

So the foundation of effective transmission of our values to our children is effective nurturing of them. Their need for acceptance and affirmation opens up their beings to us from the beginning.

Modelling

For years research has shown that non-verbal communication is more powerful than verbal.

Why is it that a child can yell for a considerable time and yet indignantly object when you raise or harden your voice in response? My children are highly sensitised to my tone of voice.

"You don't care about me at all", cries my eight-year old after a reproof.

"I do care about you, as you know. I just feel frustrated that you don't do what I ask".

"You don't care or you wouldn't talk to me like that ..."

"Don't yell at me", yells my 12-year-old.

"I'm not yelling", say I in a deliberate voice. "Yes, you are ..."

These are small examples of a pervasive truth. Actions (and tones and facial expressions and body language) speak louder than words. How we live and how we speak will make as powerful an impact as what we say.

Why raise this issue? Because our living example builds the

bones of our children's inner beings. We want to guide them through the polluted waters of our culture? Then let's examine how we plot our own course. How do our own habits measure up to the standards we set for the children?

Do our children see us indulge every desire we have that we can afford or put on credit? Do they see us connected to the poor and needy in our society?

Take the popular TV shows and movies and measure them against the Bible. Then try the buying habits and the tone of relationships in our culture. What passes the test? Our own hearts need searching. In reviewing a habit or a show ask, "Does this experience impel me towards God or does it cloud my spirit?" The children will pick up our example with a vengeance.

I know a teenager who is super-sensitised to movies, consuming reviews voraciously. He can tell you on demand what a given movie is rated and why. I have heard him comment wistfully on the viewing habits of family friends. He snoops out the video shelf in homes he visits and is baffled by what Christian families apparently watch. He asks his parents what they watch and whether they hide videos in their closet. He is doggedly defining and confirming the value set he has been offered.

As children enter adolescence, naturally they want to explore more and they will huff and puff about restrictions. Great chunks of our family communication time are spent on negotiation about viewing guidelines, money and spending habits. Complaints about movies are common fare and yet when I have collected a child early from a party to avoid a movie we deem unsuitable there has been little real objection. A show of disappointment overlying relief.

When I ask in advance about videos at a sleepover party and mention our guidelines to the host, offering to collect my child early, I sense an unspoken relaxation and respect in my child. If we stated the guidelines at home but failed to follow through in the outside world, what sort of example would that be?

We may feel invisible and inaudible to our kids but the truth is they are soaking us up. Some years ago Stephen Glenn and Jane Nelson wrote a book called *Raising Self-Reliant Children in a Self-*

Indulgent World. In it they referred to a survey in which two-thirds of young Americans expressed significant admiration for their parents and considered them among their heroes. In the *Newsweek* article mentioned earlier (May 1998, p 58) a national poll of American youth was quoted: "Teenagers named their parents as their number one heroes. Researchers say a strong parental bond is the most important protection against everything from smoking to suicide." Even in the gloom of current culture, we parents have great impact through our love and example.

Communication

Actions speak louder than words, but words speak, too. Our children need to hear us speak about our values and our reasons for them. How powerful to have a foundation of faith at this point. If we as a family are answerable to an authority outside ourselves, we have a radical starting point. The foundation will be tested, argued and maybe thrown out. Fortunately, though, the story of a life is not usually told by age 19.

Selfishness, manipulation and deceit are epidemic in the stories of our time. Biblical sexuality is a foreign concept. Physical attack is a bread-and-butter plot component. We need to challenge this in our conversation with our children. Talk about what happens between people when trust is broken. Read together what God says about attitudes between people: parents to children, children to parents and adults to authority in wider society. Talk about sex in and out of marriage (in an age-appropriate way!) The kids themselves will have many related areas raised at school. When eating and talking together at dinner, try to stimulate discussion of science and health curriculum from school. Give answers about why a certain movie is on the family's unsuitable list, why allowances aren't higher and why you will only spend a limited amount on birthday presents. Give the children some meat to chew on and let them chew, spit or swallow as they will. Of course, in your house they still have to follow the house rules. If they want to spit out your values it will have to be later in their own house.

The matter of disciplinary action for rebellious teenagers is not the subject of this article. The question here is, "Can we raise kids with God's values in a polluted society?" It's one of the hardest jobs we can tackle but the answer has to be 'Yes'. God designed families and he stands behind his design, infusing life as he has from the dawn of creation. He sees his eternal family as he shapes his children. We parents get included in his action, but our kids have more than us on their side. Just as well, eh?

THE POWER OF WORDS

*alking to my husband one evening about the day's events, I related an interaction with one of our sons. "He's hopeless. Sometimes I don't know where his head is."

What words to come out of my mouth! Our son is not hopeless at all.

Lately God has been speaking to me consistently about the power of words. You know that childhood song, "Sticks and stones might break my bones, but words can never hurt me"? Well, it's not true.

Recently I heard a woman who had survived sexual abuse. She was more than a survivor—she was an overcomer. Her summary comment on the damage done to her from the age of five years was that the greatest destructive power had come from the words spoken to her by the abuser.

Psychologists and counsellors have written about the power of self-talk for years now. Some therapies focus on identifying the inner 'tapes' played over and over in our heads and changing those tapes. Most therapies affirm that our perceptions and beliefs about our experiences are major players in both our pain and our destructive responses to life. The question is, "How do we change the tapes?"

One answer is to attack them with reason in the context of a relationship of trust. That helps. But let's take a step back and look at another level.

In Proverbs 18:21, we are told, "The tongue has the power of life and death". Strong words! In Genesis we read accounts of fathers giving life blessings to their sons. Jacob blessed each of his sons on his deathbed in Egypt. Isaac was fooled into giving Jacob the oldest son's blessing and apparently it couldn't be revoked. These blessings carried spiritual power that shaped the destinies of those blessed.

God has made us with spirits, not just bodies, thoughts and feelings. In the spiritual realm, words have power to shape reality. God spoke and the universe came into being. We, too, in a delegated way, have been given power to speak reality in the spiritual realm according to God's will.

Therefore, we must be extra careful about the words that come out of our mouths. It's so easy to say in exasperation, "You'll never learn", or "You'll never make friends", or "What's the matter with you?"

Sometimes we see such comments as lighthearted, just throwaway lines. But they are not throwaway lines. These words have more power than we might think. They don't just reflect reality, they shape it.

Blessings and cursings are real. They're not obsolete. God has given us authority to bless our children through the words we speak to them. We can also do the opposite without even realising it.

As a wife, I can bless my husband, or not. Words don't roll off his back like water off a duck. Of course not—words aren't water and he isn't a duck! He's an eternal spirit.

We, too, have been shaped by the words of others, of course. We may need some prayer and grace to forgive in order to be set free. You may become aware of words that have a hold over you. You can ask God to lift them off you. Forgive out loud whoever spoke them. Ask God to bless that person and to release you. Then watch what he will do.

If you feel convicted about the negative power of your words over your family, you can repent and renounce those words. It's best done out loud.

I prayed out loud and renounced my words over our son. Then I prayed for God to plant hope in him, to fill the void with blessing that drives out my words.

I want to grow in praying the words of scripture over my family. Let's use the words out of our mouths to bless, strengthen and release our families.

THE SPICE IN LIFE: ROMANCE, SEX AND INTIMACY IN MARRIAGE

YOUR HUSBAND'S LOVER

If an alien visited our country and wandered around the shopping centres, the alien would get the idea quickly that sex is a BIG deal here. The magazines for women are largely about other women's bodies and romances, with some how-tos for improving your own. The alien could be forgiven for assuming we spend a large proportion of our time on sex and related activities. Perhaps you do. For my part I have a confession to make. My head and my diary are mostly filled with items unrelated to sex.

In spite of the going-over that sex has had since the fall, it remains one of God's wonderful ideas. It is powerful, in personal and spiritual ways, and lots of fun. It releases tension, soothes and bonds people together. It builds us up and makes us laugh. But it requires effort. Great damage is done by that incessant parade of scantily-clad, busty, leggy, size-eight women on the magazine covers. They make female attractiveness two-dimensional, glossy and removed from the everyday world in which we live.

Real sex has to fit in after making school lunches, catching up on phone calls and handling the children. It happens in the bedroom with the day's dirty socks on the floor and a pile of books on the bedside chest. Real wives come in an astonishing array of shapes and sizes and most do not have personal trainers or a delectable collection of lingerie.

The gap between the glossy images and the real world produces a particular effect on us wives. We know the images are false. We see their emptiness and assume a higher moral ground in the privacy of our thoughts. Then, before we know it, that vague disdain has spread to sex itself as well as its distortions. The glamorised illusion has an impact. We struggle to reconcile it with what we know in experience and easily lose the plot. We think it can't be all that important to our husbands, who also see through the illusions. At least it shouldn't be—they should focus on more important matters in life, as we do.

Most husbands don't see life the same way. They are looking for some wholehearted involvement from their wives, and we neglect this at our peril. In fact, we as wives have enormous power to do our husbands good, to bless them and build them up. Good sex is a gift uniquely in our power to give. If a man is committed to Jesus and to his marriage, then he chooses to confine his sexual experience to his wife.

In short, for your husband, you are it. Whatever stimulation and fun, fantasy fulfilment and satisfaction your husband is going to have in bed is connected to you. So throw out those glamorous illusions. Your body is the one he wants. Your kisses are the ones he will respond to. Don't let the tabloids intimidate you. A wife in the bed is worth ten on the page. A man who feels that his woman is truly present and involved will appreciate whatever assets she brings to the interaction. You won't have to measure up to any ideal.

Start by creating space in the diary to spend on sex. Time spent just talking together is well worth it and time spent giving each other pleasure and attention returns good dividends. It is possible to arrange the occasional night away together (avoiding period week of course). It just has to be a priority.

Create space in your mind to spend on sex. Most of us can use a bit of warming up. Think about him when you are apart. Remember and relive good times in your past, especially good lovemaking. Are there certain clothes or underwear that make you feel more desirable? Wear them. Don't give in to feeling ridiculous if you browse in a lingerie shop. Buy yourself an occasional slinky piece for private use. He won't mind what hangs out. A little effort in his direction goes a long way and covers a multitude of sins.

Scripture talks about wives considering how to please their husbands. Here is a great starting point. Showing an interest in sex will reap a rich return. Seize the opportunity uniquely in your grasp. Your husband's lover is you.

COMMUNION

Sweet kiss,
communion wine still clinging to our lips
the mingling of soft breathing from warm throats
and fingertips touching.
Seeing into and beyond each other,
enveloped in Him,
sweet, sweet Jesus.

Your spirit holds us so gently.
We are permeable.
Your gift like a falling star
leaving shining furrows in our consciousness
and sinking bright in the centre of our being.
Your gift which is yourself
forgiveness
in us the shining effervescence
of the fallen star.

We are swept into you like a tide turning home.

Communion wine still clinging to our lips,

what more, what more is there than this?
The touching of our hands,
our lips,
our spirits.
Sweet kiss.

QUALITY TIME

After two weeks of soaring temperatures I felt like a blob of jelly on a plate oozing quietly at the edges. It was hard to show initiative. How much easier to let the days slide into each other. Let the housework slide. Let the communication slide.

When looking at the calendar earlier, I had seen the possibility of two or three evenings together with my husband. I had organised commitments with the possibility in mind of a few nights of marriage focus time. Then events changed and the window of opportunity almost closed. It would have been so easy to let it go. We were doing fine. There were no burning issues or tensions. What's more, in the heat it's so much easier to just let things go.

I got thinking about our last time away together as a couple. It had taken lots of fiddling to organise and neither of us had felt overly energetic or creative about the exercise. In fact, it had been during the Olympics and we spent a lot of time glued to the TV just like at home. Was it worth the money and effort?

Yet when we came home we were bonded a bit more closely - the conversation about friends in the deli over a slice of pizza, the walking track hidden at the end of the cul-de-sac, the cup of tea in the garden. More shared memories.

Perhaps I should make an effort.

In a momentary surge of energy I made some calls and, hey

presto! We would have one night together at home alone. I had visions of being relaxed and attractive when Allan came home. We would sit down to a lovely meal. Instead, I was just getting out of the car, hot and bedraggled, as he pulled into the drive. I unloaded the shopping I'd managed to get from the only nearby supermarket still open. We ate a simple meal - no glamour - but it was lovely.

In spite of our evening together being in the middle of a working week, we actually were greatly refreshed. In an evening and early morning we talked, swam, walked, ate, had an extended discussion of an issue that led to a decision and aired a painful grievance. Not bad for a small opportunity that nearly didn't happen.

The bottom line for me was that time together is worth the effort. There doesn't have to be a big build-up. You don't have to be struggling with a great need. Just making the time to spend as a couple is really important. It's a deep, long-term investment even with no deep and meaningfuls.

When starting a friendship you invite a person to spend time with you.

"Let's go for coffee."

"Let's see a movie."

"Come and tell me what you think I should do in my garden."

Through making time to spend with someone, you tell them you're interested in them and enjoy their company. Same message, same power years later in a marriage. By making an effort to simply spend time together you convey to each other the importance of the relationship.

Having deep talks isn't every husband's cup of tea. Everyone enjoys something, though. Reading out a joke or short article, preparing supper to eat while watching sport on TV, going for a walk or a spa or a cappuccino, playing golf or mini-golf or seeing a movie and then chatting about it over coffee afterwards - all sorts of things can become time together. Shared memories are an investment in your lives.

I'm very impressed with my brother and sister-in-law who regularly leave early for work and eat breakfast out together halfway there. Maybe the very tired husband who would never go for a walk with you might be prepared to drink his coffee after dinner on the front veranda and enjoy the night air for ten minutes before settling in for his usual evening activities.

Sex is a key element in quality time, too. We women must bear in mind that great gift we receive and give. And remember that talking doesn't always have to come before the sex!

Regular times together, whether deep and meaningful or not, are like regular deposits in a savings account. You may not even notice the automatic deduction from your working account, but there will always be worthwhile returns on the investment.

STOKING THE FIRE

'm available any time for research!"

My husband's mischievous grin surprised me no more than his generous offer. I had just told him I was planning a column on making an effort sexually as a wife—his response symbolised the issues. I answered with a smile.

Every marriage has its unique flavour, making generalisations dangerous. These days, especially, in the flux of changing gender roles, the subtleties of sex in marriage are more complex than ever. Nevertheless, it is common for sexual desire to be uneven in a couple. And the man often has the larger portion. Herein lies opportunity for tension and strain.

Nothing is more intimate than sex. It provides endless opportunity for misunderstanding, hurt and frustration, as well as pleasures and joys.

In 1 Corinthians 7:3-5, Paul wrote,

"The husband should fulfill his marital duty to his wife, and likewise the wife to her husband. The wife's body does not belong to her alone but also to her husband. In the same way, the husband's body does not belong to him alone but also to his wife. Do not deprive each other except by mutual consent and for a time."

These comments presuppose a relationship of mutual desire and hint at troubles if it is not met. If you've been married for a while, you'll know how true that is. What better way to dissolve tension and bind you close to your husband than good sex? Conversely, what sharper edge between you than frustration, resentment and misunderstanding in bed? Apparently God considers it our duty as wives to give ourselves to our husbands.

I have to confess that sometimes it has felt like a duty. But how mysterious are the unfolding seasons of marriage. At first I tried very hard, determined not to fit the stereotype of the minimally interested wife. It lasted for maybe two years—not a bad effort. Eventually, in the ebb and flow of life, I settled into a mode more genuine for me. My natural interest level was lower than my husband's. What to do?

A season of greater application, more communication and some conflict about sex followed. We had to grow and learn about this commitment we'd made to love each other. I had to learn, too, to be relaxed about my body and receiving pleasure. It was wonderful to have such an accepting and affirming husband—he didn't care that I don't have Cindy Crawford's breasts and thighs—and his is the only opinion that matters.

Then came a great step of liberation. I embraced from my heart that it is my duty to give myself to my husband. Of course, the duty is mutual and to be fulfilled in a context of respect. Nevertheless, the reality of his need was as undeniable as the reality of my need for intimacy. What a relief to decide to just say 'Yes'. Sometimes, of course, it wouldn't work, and we have always been committed to honesty. I don't pretend to offer more than I can deliver. But a general policy of 'yes' is a breath of fresh air.

Later on in 1 Corinthians (7:34), Paul continued, "An unmarried woman or virgin is concerned about the Lord's affairs: Her aim is to be devoted to the Lord in both body and spirit. But a married woman is concerned about the affairs of this world—how she can please her husband."

Although Paul was encouraging singleness, the background assumption is that a married woman expends energy considering how to please her husband. So I need to study my man, make it a conscious priority to know how he ticks. What kind of response is most precious to him? What kind of sexual initiative from me would mean most?

Nowhere else in human experience does the line between giving and receiving blur as in bed. The years have clearly shown us that in receiving pleasure from each other we give it most poignantly. What a mind God has to design such a delicate and powerful system! So, to study my man, I must study myself. To please him, I must know what pleases me. Our marriage bed must be a priority to me—even when it may not feel like one. God is as willing to empower us, as wives, in this area as in any other. He wants us to please our husbands. I think his favourite term for sex, apart from 'knowing' would be 'making love'. Because that's just what it is.

STAND BY ME

❦

*A*s a woman I wonder how men talk about us when we're not there. I know I don't like some of what I hear about men when it's just women together.

"What is it with men? He can't find his socks without me holding his hand. He asks where the salad dressing is. I tell him. Then he can't see it staring him in the face when he opens the refrigerator. Honestly, sometimes I feel like his mother, not his wife." Jokes? Maybe, but there's a sting in the tail.

Those comments coming out of my mouth would push my husband away, not pull him closer. Any discouraging remarks, any criticism, will always hurt. Sense of worth is diminished, and this is not what the marriage relationship is about. Standing side by side on our wedding day we promise to stand by our spouse from that point on. We all inhabit a world of pressure, of smaller pay-cheques and more bills, of less time to get more done. There are plenty of people out there willing to put us in a bad light or progress at our expense. Don't we all need the haven of someone to stand by us?

Two years ago we were enjoying some fun in the snow with friends from church. It was an annual event, arranged by a few giving people who arranged the meals for us all. Rostered to help prepare the dinner, I was up to my elbows in chicken thighs and sauce. Terry was the chef in charge and what a dynamo! He had definite ideas about the seasoning. "It needs a little more oregano. Would you go and get some please?" His wife smiled and agreed. I had to battle irritation with Terry a number of times that weekend. After struggling with eight enormous baking trays of slippery chicken thighs, seasoned quite nicely thank you, I could have let the oregano slip by. When he gave me a task and then efficiently did it himself anyway, I had to breathe slowly. Hannah, his wife, just worked with his style and made the system flow. I noticed.

It would have been easy to undermine Terry with no more than a roll of the eyes. Hannah never once rolled her eyes. She showed only affection and respect. Lately I have noticed that she has taken time out from ministry in the church for some spiritual renewal. Just the other day Terry was visiting us and mentioned how he had decided to drop out of some church obligations for a while in order to invest more in Hannah and the children. He speaks of her with such love and respect. Maybe the stresses of living with a dynamo are getting faced and worked on. In private there have probably been many tensions and hard, painful talks. I heard something about a counsellor. Hannah is a real and honest person, just discreet and gracious in her talk. They are a united front to their world, a loyal unit.

In my own marriage our goal is the same. We've made a pact that we will never run each other down in public. In fact, we do not share anything negative or embarrassing about each other without specific permission. It gives us security. I trust my husband completely in his social conversations, whether I'm present or not. We can fight things out as much as we need in private. Honesty is a high value for our relationship, but we can always count on each other's loyalty.

In our Australian culture of knocking—even showing affection by running people down—we are at constant risk of discouraging our spouses, of eroding their courage and hope. Is this our aim? It seems rather like biting off our noses to spite our faces. Once we're married we're stuck together and where one goes so does the other. If your husband is growing more secure and building his courage and pursuing his dreams, that must be better for you as his wife. Of course, we all need to hear and process input from life. We need to face our faults and change, but it isn't the spouse's job to be the daily voice of revelation in this regard. Being married should mean you always have someone on your side, not on your back.

We rightly hear much about rekindling and building romance in marriage, but it's hard to enjoy romance in a house without a roof. Loyalty is the roof on the house of our relationship. Let's make it secure and then build the fire inside.

KEEPING SHORT ACCOUNTS

*R*ecently my husband and I had a rare opportunity. We found ourselves free to go to a prayer day together—for the whole day! I had been looking forward to it eagerly. As we prepared to leave in the morning, though, I was aware of feeling just slightly wrong-footed emotionally, too easily irritated.

As we drove across the city in the fresh morning light I struggled to hold our two travel mugs of coffee steady. He didn't take my preferred route and our thinking didn't match as we discussed last week. When we arrived, I opened my side door too wide and hit the car parked alongside us. That kind of thing really frustrates Allan. He rolled his eyes. I was grateful to the Lord that the other car had a rubber strip, and no, upon investigation the little red mark on their door hadn't come from me after all.

I trotted into the church building heavy-hearted. "This is no good at all." Fortunately, I was awake enough to realise this was a spiritual attack. It was so petty, yet so obvious it was almost ludicrous. I would have been pretty thick to miss it. Maybe some demons at a loose end were having a bit of silly fun.

As we settled into the auditorium, I slipped my hand through Allan's arm.

"I'm sorry for all the ways I irritate you."

"I'm sorry for all the ways I irritate you, too."

Ah—such a lovely, warm feeling of peace. We had a wonderful day of prayer.

This episode is a trivial one, yet it reminded me of the power of keeping short accounts in our marriage. That day was too precious to be compromised. We wanted to be clean and receptive. Yet every day is precious - what day can we spare to fritter away with unnecessary frustration?

In Ephesians 4:26-27, Paul warns us "In your anger do not sin. Do not let the sun go down while you are still angry, and do not give the devil a foothold." He warned us clearly about letting anger and resentment fester. It gives the devil a foothold. It will make us sick in the end.

Tension and conflict have two sides, of course. I can be distanced from my husband both by feeling he has hurt me and by my guilt over hurting him.

In the first case expression of the hurt is needed. What married woman breathes who has never felt taken for granted, misunderstood, wrongly criticised or hurt? If we sit on those thoughts and feelings, they grow. It's amazing how much corroborating evidence we will collect for our internal accusations. The mental posture of victim springs up with ready vitality. You'd think we all took a course in it at high school.

Hardness soon gains a foothold in us and influences all incoming information. We develop internal habits of defence, and withdraw, even if slightly, from spontaneity, warmth and intimacy. Naturally, if I'm occupying myself with feeling hard done by, I will defend myself from further hurt.

Open acknowledgment of the hurt must find voice. The boil must be lanced. I have been long in learning this lesson. By natural inclination I'm definitely a hoarder, and early in our marriage I tended to sit on feelings and hurts.

There are so many conflicting thoughts and feelings about expressing anger among Christians. God has slowly been working me out of that pattern, and I know deep in my being that open expression can bring light and life. Tucking resentments away in corners infects one bit of you after another. Who wants to end up a bag of pus?

If I have hurt Allan, the key again is honest acknowledgment. On sensing our husbands have been hurt, upset or frustrated by us, we have a choice. We can be open and hear, or we can bend our energy to justifying ourselves. As long as we're busy with self-justification, no progress in the relationship takes place. There's no harm in reflection on ourselves and our husbands in order to understand. However, the heart posture must be one of openness. We have to stop justifying ourselves if we want to live in harmony and flourish as a couple.

I want to be open to receive from God, not now and again, but constantly. One of the practical steps to that position is keeping short accounts with my husband. The air must be clear, and the channels must be flowing freely between us.

THE FINER THINGS OF LIFE

I turned to lift my foot up the last step into our bedroom. It had been a long day with unexpected demands. I was looking forward to communion with my bed.

What was that? On the carpet at the entrance to the room lay a brown envelope. I picked it up. Recognising my sister-in-law's handwriting, I put the envelope on my pillow to enjoy later.

Teeth cleaned and snuggled under the quilt alone (my husband was away), I opened the envelope and read her message. How delightful to finish the day with sweet words of appreciation and encouragement. My sister-in-law has a gift for encouraging people. I was lecturing, and she had come, at short notice, to spend time with the children when my other plans had fallen through. Her offer was a gift—her life is already lived in the fast lane, without me adding to it. Then she left a card to express appreciation for me!

All week I have savoured that little bonus gift. Sweet words are such a lovely present. It got me thinking about how precious little gestures can be.

In the rush and bustle of everyday family life, that's easy to forget. After years of marriage, how easily I can take my husband for granted. (I have my turns at feeling taken for granted as well, of course.)

The daily routine becomes familiar and full. So many little

matters require attention, especially when children are involved. I find it important to include my husband in the loop of domestic decisions. Should the children be allowed to go to the Royal Adelaide Show with friends? Can one son sleep over on Friday night? Exactly how much money should we give each child for a meal while at the Show? How about the child who doesn't want to go? Should he have equivalent money to spend in other ways? Is it too much to invite two different families for meals this week? Who should be given priority and invited first? How will we get grand-parents to the concert next week?

When I make a run of decisions without communicating with my husband, I eventually come to grief. Sometimes one of the decisions is too important to be made alone. Or we begin to feel separated from each other.

With busy schedules and time apart due to work, it's not easy, though. Such issues can soak up precious time together.

That's where my lovely brown envelope comes in. Do I make an effort to express my appreciation for my husband just for the sake of it? It's not hard to spend a few minutes adding a note to his lunch box or making a call during the day to touch base. Heart-shaped chocolates wrapped in gold or red foil can be found in all sorts of stores. A short foot massage or back rub before bed is nothing short of delicious. And, of course, sweet words.

"Thank you for providing for us."

"Your long fingers are so lovely."

"I enjoy looking into your eyes as much as when we first met."

When I have time, I like looking at romantic and sexy cards (appropriate, of course!) to give my husband when it isn't his birth-day. I love to meet his eyes and smile over the dinner table. I love to linger ever so briefly over the coming-home kiss. It only takes a few seconds longer to stroke hair or cheek, but it feels quite different.

One of the biggest gifts to many husbands is making time for sex —willing, involved sex. My goal is to think every day of some little (or big) thing I can do to tell him I love him.

It all originates with God, of course. He didn't design us to simply function, living out our lives in a drab and grey existence. He gave us the capacity to appreciate the finer things of life: the beauty that surrounds us, the extravagance of colour, sound, taste, touch and smell.

Respect and commitment, discipline and clear communication are the substance, the bones of a marriage. But a wink across the room, a caress when passing, the tenderness in bed—these give the colour and pizazz.

IN IT FOR THE LONG HAUL

"*Y*ou've brought me flowers! How sweet!"

"I know how much you love them."

This conversation took place at our front door. I was the one arriving with the flowers, though, and my husband's welcoming smile was as wicked as his greeting. The flowers came from my mother's garden, and, in spite of his cheeky remark, my husband knew perfectly well I wouldn't be bringing them for him. I have no doubt he was thinking about our rather chequered history with flowers.

It would no more occur to me to give Allan flowers than to fly to the moon, but I like receiving them myself. The fact is we're different; we respond to different cues and we hope for different things. And yet we're best friends.

How do you celebrate the differences rather than allow them to drive you apart? How do you build on the strengths? These issues need a husband's perspective as well as a wife's, I invited my husband to join me in a dialogue.

Allan: "For starters, let me make it clear that I married you for your body."

Me: "I don't believe you."

Allan: "Well, the truth is that I was attracted to you for other reasons. And it's a good thing, too, because we certainly wouldn't have made it through 25 years if sex was the only thing on the menu."

Me: "That's for sure. From the beginning it was wonderful to be good friends. I felt like we would never run out of things to talk about. Do you remember how we decided early in our marriage not to let unresolved issues fester?"

Allan: "Yes. In our parents' generation we saw couples with marital issues so tense that neither party could safely talk about them. We were determined not to have no-go zones in our marriage."

Me: "It hasn't always been easy to follow through on that. Sometimes we had to choose talking over sleeping. Talking to each other is still one of the most important things to me. It's just as true today as when we started out together. I feel very loved when you spend time talking to me."

Allan: "Communicating with you is an important safety valve for me. It helps that you're a good listener. I don't feel judged when I tell you what's going on. And yet I know you'll keep me honest, with myself and in my relationships with other people. There are times when I over-react and need you to reel me in."

Me: "I find you a good listener, too. It would be impossible to measure the impact of that on our relationship and my wellbeing. I appreciate that you don't always have to solve my problems. Usually I don't need you to solve them for me, but it's so crucial to be heard and cared about. If you want me to be putty in your hands in bed, that's one way to make it happen."

Allan: "Being a bit slow, it took me at least a decade to learn that I didn't have to always find a solution to your problems. Often a sympathetic hug is all you're really looking for. I try to take your feelings seriously, though. I've discovered, of course, that there are times when you shouldn't take your own feelings too seriously, especially at certain times of the month. 'Big picture' analyses of your life are banned during pre-menstrual week!"

Me: "Yes, I remember being quite put out when you would downplay my negativity because of PMS. But over time I've learnt to be more detached from those moods myself. Your acceptance and respect has made that possible. If I felt written off generally as an irrational woman, we would not be where we are today."

Allan: "Wouldn't it be nice if we were always considerate and rational? Being sinful people, though, we've had our share of clashes. Always your fault, of course."

Me: "Of course, dear."

Allan: "What has most of our conflict been about from your point of view?"

Me: "Feeling misunderstood or unappreciated. I need to feel cherished. Even the little things matter to me, like when you smile at me across a room, or stroke my hair, or touch me affectionately when walking past."

Allan: "Guilty as charged. Sometimes I'm simply lazy or too self-absorbed to pay attention to what you're feeling."

Me: "It sure kills intimacy to feel taken for granted."

Allan: "I do take you too much for granted. Sometimes, though, when you're wrestling with a martyr complex, I think the issues have as much to do with you as with me."

Me: "I agree, though it hasn't been easy for me to see it that way. After all, who wants to take responsibility for their own sinfulness? Feeling hard done by can be a very satisfying indulgence. What's the problem at those times?"

Allan: "I hate being placed in a no-win situation. I remember when the kids were younger you felt like I didn't do enough to help with the morning routine. One day you erupted, and told me you were sick of getting up four kids, making their lunches and organising them for school while I slept in till the last possible moment. I said I couldn't understand why you didn't ask for help instead of suffering in silence. You replied that you weren't my mother - I should be big enough to see for myself what needed to be done with my own kids, not wait around for you to organise me as well."

Me: "I bet you were grateful to receive my honest communication."

Allan: "Yes, and all pigs were fed and ready to fly. I was ashamed because you were right. But when I offered to take on specific responsibilities to lighten your load, you didn't want to give them up. So I felt caught. I suggested you were more interested in feeling like a martyr than actually receiving any help. And I said that next time I'd appreciate an early warning system instead of you playing out the rope until you knew I had enough to hang myself."

Me: "The big growth point for me is to get my feelings out. I need to let you know what I want instead of stewing and expecting you to be a mind reader."

Allan: "The only thing that changed in the end was that I took over plaiting the girls' hair each morning. It felt like a token effort to me, but it seemed to satisfy you. I think getting it into the open was half the battle."

Me: "What has most of our conflict been about from your point of view?"

Allan: "Sex has been an issue, of course. Especially in the early years of our marriage."

Me: "What a surprise!"

Allan: "There've been times when I've despaired of you ever understanding how I operate. I feel close to you when our sexual relationship is in good shape. For you it seems to be the other way round - good sex flows out of feeling close to me."

Me: "Yes, we've tripped on this over the years. I think it's a bit more subtle, though. I know you need to feel close to me, too - you're not just looking for a sex object. For my part, I've learnt that sometimes it's better to have the sex first and the talk later."

Allan: "And I've had to learn that sex doesn't have to always happen when I want it."

Me: "It's been good to become more relaxed about this issue. I've needed to learn to trust you and not put my needs first."

Allan: "That's been the challenge for me, too. God has used it as a growth point in my life. When I'm in pain, I'm a bit more open to spiritual surgery."

Me: "Yes. Our differences in sex have been deep entry points for God's grace. He seems to be busy in the bedroom."

Allan: "Now that I'm older, it's easier to get sex into perspective. Maybe I'll even get better at the important things. Like flowers!"

THE PLUNGE

The sand is gritty between my fingertips
but warm, so warm.
How many suns have shone and set over this beach,
slowly heating these ancient grains?
Too many to count.
This afternoon I am lying in it, lying in the warmth,
soaking up the beauty.

There are so many beauties to savour here.
I like to dream of them, shimmering,
hazily impinging on me.
No effort is required to lie here and imagine the rock pools
    and caves
and hidden nooks out there ...
to float from one to another in my mind's eye
like seaweed on the surface of the water.
This is warm and wonderful.

But not enough.
Now I must move, change.
There is more than such general, passive beauty.

Donning mask and snorkel,
I plunge beneath the surface of the ocean,
the close, vibrant, vivid undersea.
...Shocking
......tingling
.........cold
All is pulsing and
silent except for my heart and breath.
Can I move with my loud breath pressing upon me?

Yes
Steady
... kick
......steady
.........glide
Now my breath is steady,
the measured rhythm of the universe.

Fluid brilliance a million miles from the beach ...
Liquid aquamarine a million miles from the air above.
Enfolding
Liberating
I can roll and glide and dart in any direction,
and the beauty glows everywhere.
This beauty just for me.
I didn't guess the pool was so deep,
the rocks so intricate,
the weed so vivid green.
What incredible complexity in every nook and fold of these
*   ancient,*
secret surfaces. These hidden rocks have absorbed countless
*   suns too.*
All is richer, more golden, as though stored-up warmth were
*   being*
gently slow-released.

Here beneath the surface lies another world of detail.

Let me take time to swim around this pool.
Let me peer at rocks and shells and plants,
turn over a white fan shell in my hand.
It is one of a million on this coastline,
but so stunningly beautiful.
I never knew.

I must take time.
The details are so important,
so different at this range.

Love is like this.

To love is to know,
to consider the details of the other.
To turn them over in your hand.
The details are so important,
and different at close range.

Adam knew Eve,
and the human family began.

I will know you, my love,
This beauty just for me.

Yes ... I will plunge

Yes ... I will swim

I will know this beauty.
I will swim.

INTIMACY WITH GOD

FRESH WATER

ondering our family life while cleaning up in the kitchen, I was struck again by how quickly our years together are flying by. It didn't feel like that when the children were little. Now they're teenagers, though, it seems like we're in the home stretch of hands-on parenting. It's sad sometimes and scary.

On this particular autumn day the sadness centred on one thing. I wished we'd made more focus on praying together. My mind wandered to the renewing that God is doing in me. I started sharing my kitchen sink thoughts with him.

Jesus promised that rivers of living water would flow out of the inner beings of people who relate to him (John 7:37-39). Now, that's a fascinating thought. He said if we're thirsty we should go to him and drink. I take that as a promise that our thirst will be quenched. He also gave an extra promise of living water flowing out of us to others.

Well, he's got my attention. I definitely want to be fulfilled and satisfied with my life. I want to be someone who helps propel others into the same fulfilment.

If there's a queue for living water that gushes out of the inner being, then I'm lining up. Forget the housework and the church committees for a bit. I have a more important priority today.

What an adventure to live life by following Jesus' Spirit who gushes out. He is full of vitality and life and surprises. He's full of ideas.

As I pondered our family in the kitchen that day, I felt that God released an idea to me. The idea was very simple: "Why not start a family prayer time once a week?" Along with it was a definite thought that we should start a weekly family night as well, just for fun, separate from the prayer time.

Now there's nothing earth-shattering about these ideas. People have written about them in books and magazines for years. We'd never done either regularly, though. And if a friend had suggested them to me that day I would probably have reacted immediately: "It won't work, we've left it too late." 'Family night' seems like something you do with younger children.

However, when God releases an idea, it's amazing. The content was not new, but my reaction was, "Yes, such a simple plan and a good one." Logic said that the kids wouldn't be interested and that life's too full anyway. My heart said, "Yes. It's a good idea." Ideas from God are different. There's more to them than content.

Along with the thought came a surge of hope. A renewed love for my job as a mother warmed me. I received the patience to proceed at God's pace, and a release of faith that he would do it. All this in a flash! Now that's what I call a life-giving idea. It was a sip from the well of living water.

We embarked on weekly prayer times in the morning before school, and weekly family nights as well. There was some eye-rolling at first. Occasionally I still see a roll. There's no pressure to come to the prayer time and we don't all make it. Maybe if we'd started younger it would have been better. We do strongly encourage everyone to be at family night.

I generally prepare something a bit special for breakfast after the prayer time. I'm amazed at how naturally this all fits in. We take turns at choosing the activity for family night. We've watched movies, played cards, played charades, gone out for milk-shakes. There isn't uniform enthusiasm, but it happens.

I believe that these ideas came from God and that they're valuable for us as a family at the moment. One of the confirmations to me is the patience he has given me to let them unfold. If he's started them, he'll achieve what he wants with them. When we miss, that's OK; we'll just come back next time. I don't get discouraged at grumbling or mumbling, either. I just keep making the pancake mix, turning up for prayer, cooking the special tea and putting aside the evening once a week.

Some prayer times have been great. Some family nights have been great. I'm thankful to Jesus for all his promises and I keep lining up for that fresh living water.

GLOWING WITH HEALTH

*R*emember in Sunday school making a little stretcher out of a matchbox? A paralysed pipe-cleaner man would be gently lowered through the roof of the shoebox right in front of a white pipe-cleaner figure of Jesus, busy teaching the throngs.

"Friend, your sins are forgiven", says Jesus, unfazed. The Pharisees get hot under the collar about Jesus taking God's authority and forgiving sins. Jesus simply says to the man on the stretcher, "Get up, take up your bed and walk."

The pipe-cleaner man jumps up and jigs around. He is healed. He can walk. He is forgiven.

This account in Luke 5 links forgiveness and healing. We're not told whether the man's sin directly caused his paralysis or what sins were forgiven. Given the way Jesus responded, though, many commentators believe that on this occasion the sickness was indeed related to the man's sin. Jesus didn't generalise it to all paralysed legs, though.

Many biblical statements connect spiritual and physical health. Proverbs 3:5,6 provides an often-quoted encouragement to trust in God rather than our own understanding. But the next verses were less well known to me until recently. "Do not be wise in your own eyes; fear the Lord and shun evil. This will bring health to your body and nourishment to your bones" (Proverbs 3:7,8).

I've been relishing The Message lately; Peterson's paraphrase puts it like this: "Don't assume that you know it all. Run to God! Run from evil! Your body will glow with health, your very bones will vibrate with life."

I feel better all over when I'm actively listening for God's voice and staying open to him. I sleep better, eat better and work out of a sense of peace. My stomach isn't tense and I'm far less likely to get headaches or indigestion. Friends regularly confirm this experience and I find myself thinking about Proverbs 3:5-8 often.

To understand health it helps to know something about stress. The body's stress response is a sophisticated physiological defence system that helps us handle life's challenges. It is a state of adrenaline arousal, the body mobilising resources to meet a demand. Stress is necessary for life.

However, we often live in an over-stressed state, leading to all kinds of health problems. Heart rate and blood pressure increase, stomach acid is secreted and muscles tense up. Our immune systems and natural anti-pain and anti-anxiety systems are suppressed. Specialists assert that we are over-stimulated. Consequently, we have incapacitated some of our resources for maintaining health.

People who live habitually with a body mobilised for action are vulnerable to a range of health problems, including headache, backache, nervous tics and heart disease. Moreover, the triggers to the stress response are almost endless. Anything counts that annoys, worries, hurries, angers, frustrates, challenges, scares or excites us.

The inner triggers are the deadliest. Worry, anxiety, resentment and frustration all produce stress responses in the body, but may not lead to confrontation or resolution.

Here's where the dynamic link to sin comes in. Rehearsing the ills done to us will cause tension. Revisiting criticisms we harbour will cause tension. Worrying will cause tension. Eventually the tension does its damage: we have recurring headaches, sleep poorly, and crave chocolate and coffee to keep our sleep-deprived bodies going. And so the cycle continues.

Jesus promises peace. He offers rest for our souls. We must live in daily relationship with him, giving him our fears and worries, releasing to him our angers, bitterness and frustration.

"Run to God! Run from evil! Your body will glow with health."

"Bring it on!" we say.

The paralysed man is something different. Paralysis is more than a stress response. James 5:15,16 says that if you are sick "the prayer offered in faith will make you well; the Lord will raise you up. If you have sinned, you will be forgiven. Therefore confess your sins to each other and pray for each other so that you may be healed. The prayer of a righteous person is powerful and effective."

Judith suffered from back pain for years. It came on gradually but was definitely getting worse. Her quality of life was markedly affected and she needed pain relief to get through the day. She was a believer, but felt greatly hindered by an unsatisfactory marriage. Her children were independent now, and with time on her hands she focused more on her problems.

She decided to visit a healing prayer centre. How could it hurt? As she opened herself to the Holy Spirit, she felt convicted of wrong attitudes to her husband. She was hanging on to criticisms of him, rehearsing resentment about their relationship. When Judith confessed and received God's forgiveness, something amazing happened. Her back pain went away.

Just last weekend I chatted with a pastor who spends substantial time praying with people. He reported several instances of women with back pain and bad attitudes to their husbands who had been healed. Once again, this does not mean all women with back pain resent their husbands! However, Jesus still says, "Friend, your sins are forgiven", and people still get freed from pain and disability.

I try to keep short accounts with God. Confession, forgiveness and cleansing emerge as basic elements of prayer and healing, over and over again.

I frequently ask God to bring to light anything hidden that needs exposure. If I am in pain, I usually pray that way. God then has permission to reveal any relevant sins. I don't try hard to dredge them up; God is well able to do the job. My part is openness.

James wrote that we should confess our sins and pray for each other. There is more power here than we usually tap into.

Sometimes we need more focused help. I'm fortunate in knowing a pastor experienced in healing prayer. He isn't part of my denomination, but is a great resource. Interest in healing prayer is increasing; you may find someone trustworthy in your area. Some Christian health professionals also address spiritual issues.

Jesus heals. His desire is for wholeness and there is an intimate link between our connection to him and our wellbeing. We move towards health as we daily live a life of trust. Proverbs 3 is only one reference to this truth. As we trust ourselves to God, we experience peace that reverberates through our whole systems.

In areas of specific need there can be a connection to hurt and to sin. We need to let God lead us into both giving and receiving forgiveness. God is the great healer and will set our feet on the path to wholeness when we ask him.

WISHING AND HOPING AND
THINKING AND PRAYING

*S*o goes the old song, as if they were the same. Are they?
I don't think so.

From earliest memories most of us have blown out candles on a birthday cake and made a wish. Don't you wonder what your children wish for? I like to know because it gives me a window on their hearts. Out of the well of dreams and appetites all sorts of wishes get pulled up. Wishes reveal what is in us.

I wish my children wouldn't argue and I wish I didn't get grumpy in pre-menstrual week. Johnny wishes he could have more time on computer games and Mary wishes she didn't have to clean her room. Do these qualify as hopes? No. They show what is in me and Johnny and Mary.

When we pray, are we expressing our wishes or our hopes to God? Maybe it's both. I think we often start from wishes, like wishing on a star or lighting a candle and screwing up our insides to try to make something good happen. But we know wishes often don't come true.

In this book the matter of disappointment has frequently raised its head. Disappointment is an opportunity for learning. When things don't go our way we need to re-examine the way we're going. Life with God in the real world forces many such re-examinations.

Pain propels us from wishes to something deeper as we progress forward.

If wishes show what is in us, what do hopes show? Where does hope come from? That's an easy one. Our hope comes from God and what he has done in Jesus. We are hoping for a new heaven and new earth. We are hoping for Jesus to come back and set all to right in the mess we've made. We are hoping to be pure and free and close to him forever. Why do we have these hopes? Because we know God's promises. Our hopes are based on God, on reality outside of and beyond us.

Just as Mary's wish not to clean her room doesn't relate to the reality of her lifestyle, so many of our wishes and prayers don't relate to the eternal reality we live in. Expressing our wishes to God is a good place to start, but we must expect God to respond and interact with us about them. Mary's mother will do the same about her room. The chances of Mary having a lovely tidy room in the long term without her needing to clean it are very slim. Wishes open communication.

However, in order to know what we can count on and persevere in hoping for, we must hear the wider reality. God wants to move us from our wishes (expressing internal fantasies) to deep solid hope in him. When Johnny doesn't get his wish for unrestricted time on computer games he is quite likely to feel his parents don't love him. Even if he doesn't feel it he may well say it. The focus then gets up close and personal in a most unhelpful way. Similarly, when the wishes we have expressed to God are not fulfilled it's so easy to retreat into feeling he isn't real or isn't loving. Maybe we feel we're the problem. We're defective. Doubt springing from disappointment has a number of poisonous leaks. More likely God wants to deepen us. He wants us to know him better, and how can we without interaction?

Hebrews 11:1 says "faith is being sure of what we hope for and certain of what we do not see". The ancients were commended for it, and there follows a list of what they did in faith. Faith is action, the tangible outworking of hope. As we grasp the eternal reality outside of and beyond ourselves, we are released to work. We pursue what we hope for. Then we know him more deeply. If wishes show what is in us, then hopes show what is in God.

So the confusion and pain of disappointment is fodder for ongoing dialogue with God. Sin sneaks in to distort and divert. We are so prone to idolatrous hope founded on illusions about ourselves and the world. God wants to reveal himself in that pain. Then the pool of wishes and dreams transforms to reflect reality, and hope grows deep in the soul. Hope that brings strength to weather the storms of disappointment.

THE TEARS THAT FALL

"*B*lessed are the tears that fall, that clean the windows of
the soul
Usher in a change of heart, and bring the joy that
angels know",

sings Bryan Duncan on his album *Anonymous Confessions of a
Lunatic Friend*. Lately I've found my mind wandering back to these
haunting lines. Perhaps because I've felt like crying lately. One day
this week I couldn't stop. All morning, while driving around in my
van the tears flowed down my cheeks. I wasn't quite sure of all they
expressed but I couldn't stop them and I blessed the designer of
tissue boxes that fit snugly into our dashboard. It wasn't even that
time of the month.

In Ecclesiastes 3 Solomon wrote

"There is a time for everything

and a season for every activity under heaven

... a time to weep and a time to laugh ..."

Yes, there is a time for both, and flat indeed is the life without
weeping and without laughing. It's interesting that many people at
times of spiritual renewal experience both extended sessions of
weeping and of laughing from the Spirit.

Jesus wept in the face of death and its haughty conquest of the
life of his friend Lazarus—so deeply untrue from God's eternal

perspective. And God's people wept in their ancient captivity (Psalm 126). He heard them and turned their tears into songs of joy.

What do tears say? Most basically they say, "I hurt". Children in pain run to mother or father crying. When we're grown-up our hurts get more complex. Tears might come from

- frustration—"I'm blocked and I can't stand it"
- sadness—"This just hurts inside"
- disappointment—"I had hoped for so much more"
- grief—"The world is so far from the truth, from what is right and good"
- loss—"I'm wounded. Something precious is lost. I'm poorer"

and more.

Like most things, tears are usually a mixture of messages. Disappointment merges into sadness with a dash of frustration. What begins as a true, deep grief for our lost world extends into a self-centred fit of the miseries, and, of course, the other way round. At least, so it is with me.

In all these states there is a build-up of generalised feeling.

Insomuch as emotion is electro-chemical, it's like being over-charged inside. We need to discharge sometimes. I know when I'm in a turmoil or confusion of feelings there is a great release in tears. Rationally this release doesn't make much sense. Liquid oozing out of eye-sockets, a blocked nose and a headache don't change the issues at stake. But the release and relief are undeniable. Discharging the build-up of emotional energy allows us to tackle the issues differently.

Tears do seem to wash the windows of the soul. They create a special kind of quietness that allows the ushering in of a change of heart. Bryan Duncan's song goes on:

"Blessed are the tears that fall, that wash the stains of life away.

Forgiven and forgotten now, a new creation's here to stay."

The incredible power of the cross, of forgiveness, is what brings new creation—yet somehow the emotional discharge of tears often helps me to feel the cleansing freshly in a given situation. Tears help clear the way to think about how being a new creation is to be lived out here and now.

Precious indeed are the times when sadness or frustration extend into true grief, for those outside of me, for myself, or both. I can remember particular occasions, even from years ago, when there has been a sense of my tears counting somehow.

I think of tears that seem to come from quite outside myself. In private worship sometimes I am suddenly overwhelmed by tears that feel clearly intercessory. They come and go beyond my choice or emotions and I am left with a beautiful and surprising sense of being the Spirit's home. It shouldn't be surprising, of course.

From sheer self-pity to cleansing grief, God takes our tears seriously.

"Blessed are those who mourn", Jesus said, "for they shall be comforted."

When I cry and when I pray I often think of the picture in Revelation 5:8 of the golden bowls full of incense, which are the prayers of the saints. Maybe I'm wrong, but I can't help but think of those prayers containing many tears.

Take our tears, Lord. Make them count. Wash our souls. Thank you.

RENEWAL

We will not knock on your door today.
No, we will not come.
You are at home and quiet
but we will not come.

Today is a cleaning day,
warm and windy.
Your crumpled, rumpled soul has been
stripped from its bed,
washed,
shaken with a flourish in the sun.
Your heavy soul has been
stretched flat and taut,
pegged up on the line
like a stiff, white flag
in a kindergarten collage.

This is a day to be at home and quiet.
We will not bother you,
resting limp without your soul.

Blow, wind, blow.

BETTER THAN A KIT-KAT

J hadn't spoken to my friend for some weeks when we found ourselves together in the coffee line after church. It was delicious.

"How have you been? I've been praying for you. In fact, you've been especially on my mind."

"Really? Thank you. Well, in that case, let me tell you something that happened just last week." She pointed towards a free table.

We sat down with our coffee. That was a gift in itself; my teenagers usually come for a stream of negotiations about social activities, and my friend's pre-schoolers are very bright, energetic and demanding.

She told me about how she'd been exhausted by mothering the previous weekend. She described herself as completely wrung out. After a very solid few days with children consistently arguing back and her feeling like a policeman, by Sunday night she'd had it. She put the children to bed, shut the bathroom door and sank into a warm bath. She felt ragged and empty and a failure at mothering, having brought a bunch of defiant, selfish, unmanageable people into the world.

Being the wise woman she is, her response was to cry out to God from the bathtub. She needed him. And she felt that he answered her in such a beautiful way. As she soaked in the warm suds, a picture came clearly to her mind of three small stalks in a paddock. The sun shone, the rain fell, and the stalks grew. Then she saw a big stalk next to them and knew it was her. She sensed that the little stalks were her children, and that God was speaking to her.

He assured her that he was in control, and that she had to nurture her children. She needed to keep on nurturing and all would be well. By the end of the bath she felt renewed and encouraged and very close to Jesus. The heavy layer of failure washed down the plughole.

It made me think of Isaiah 40:11: "He tends his flock like a shepherd. He gathers the lambs in his arms and carries them close to his heart; he gently leads those that have young."

Jesus was gently leading my friend, who also 'has young'. I have known love like that from him in mothering, too. Time and time again.

My friend received from Jesus because she asked, of course. She chose to stop and spend time with him. She could have recited her woes over and over to herself or her husband or a friend. She could have escaped into a movie, leaving all the underlying tension and exhaustion unaddressed.

In Matthew 11:28-30, Jesus invites us to relate to him: "Come to me, all you who are weary and burdened, and I will give you rest. Take my yoke upon you and learn from me, for I am gentle and humble in heart, and you will find rest for your souls. For my yoke is easy and my burden is light."

In mothering, as in every part of life, Jesus wants to be the source of our life. He wants to be the well of living water that we drink from. To me, that means life and creativity, energy and inspiration, hope and vision and the will to go on. He wants to be all this to us. When he told us to take his yoke and learn from him, I'm sure he didn't only mean us to observe him as a model and copy him. He never was a mother. We couldn't copy him exactly. He was talking about relating to him, drawing life from him. It's all tied up with him living inside us by his Spirit. What resources we have for living and mothering!

We do have to choose to spend time with Jesus, though. We must be quiet with him. It might mean listening to music, taking a child for a walk in the stroller, having a bath or journalling. We might need help from husband or friend to have a little period of solitude, but planned times aren't always the best ones. If our attitude is to confide honestly in Jesus, and our expectation is that he will respond, we will find wonderful rest and refreshment.

YOU DON'T LOSE YOUR FOOTING
ON YOUR KNEES

I once heard a pastor from California quote an interesting statistic. He said that the current divorce rate in the US is around one in two. However, the divorce rate for couples who regularly pray together is one in 1,050. I don't know his source, but it's an astonishing figure. What a contrast! I know which odds I prefer.

It got me thinking about our experience with parenting lately and what God has been impressing on us. Parenting involves service and communication, setting boundaries, establishing consequences, following through, striving for consistency, affirming our children, and on and on. Lately, however, I've been struck by a deep sense that the primary work in parenting is prayer.

All the other things we do and struggle to do are essential, of course; this is not an either/or situation. However, in my heart I call out to God for my children.

As a couple, my husband and I are praying together for our children. We discuss them and how to handle things, sure. In fact, these teenage years seem to require a huge amount of discussing and sorting through. But the undergirding dynamic is prayer.

Ultimately, God is the only one who can reach a person's soul. The power for change comes from him. Our role as parents is crucial but no power for life actually comes from us.

As James Dobson has said, "Parenting isn't for cowards". The situations that arise in guiding the growth of an adolescent person are not simple. There are plenty of head-scratchers. A couple of situations in our home in the last few weeks have stretched us uncomfortably. Then a child has surprised us by making a good choice where all the indicators pointed the other way. We've had such a sense of God answering prayer.

When we pray, we not only see God's hand move in the person we pray for, but we also open ourselves to him changing us. He has promised to give wisdom without reproach to those who ask (James 1:5). Family relationships certainly require wisdom. I need time directly with God and time with my husband to stay clear, humble and focused in mothering.

Maybe one day there'll be a study that compares life outcomes for children who were prayed for with children who were not. Maybe we'll have to wait for heaven for that.

One thing struck me about the original quote concerning couples who pray together. The pastor didn't say that couples do better if they go to church together, or share Christian beliefs and values. He said it about couples who pray together. There is something so powerful, so dynamic, so humbling about praying together.

On the whole, as Christians we are good at saying we will pray, at intending to pray, at thinking about praying, at assuming each other is praying. When we see couples who seem united and active in the church, it's easy to assume they have a strong prayer life together. Not necessarily so.

In fact, it's very hard to have prayer together as couples. If you surveyed your church and everyone was honest, you'd probably get a surprise. Simple, out loud prayers with someone with whom you are intimate are hard to sustain. Maybe Satan especially attacks them because of their power. Maybe that's why we feel stilted and weird, and circumstances conspire against us praying as couples.

In Matthew 18:19, we have the promise that "if two of you on earth agree about anything you ask for, it will be done for you by my Father in heaven". Let's resist the pressures and make praying together as couples a reality.

BREATHE, JUST BREATHE

⌘

*S*ome people just have no idea of time. Every family has one —the person who goes to the toilet and requires a search party to be retrieved. As a boy, my husband would get lost between the back door and the bin reading the newspapers the rubbish was wrapped in.

We have a couple of dreamers like that. In our better moments we call it "having a rich inner life".

Family schedules are complex these days. People who aren't ready on time cause constant stress. It's not easy to let the culprit learn by suffering natural consequences, either. Everyone else suffers at least as much.

Lately I've been handling this matter more calmly in our family. The days don't always begin with a tirade in the car on the way to school. I've been trying to prompt earlier and just breathe.

Recently, however, I was brought up abruptly. One of our daughters had been invited to spend the weekend away with family friends. She was due at our friends' house by 5pm Friday. Two other children needed to be dropped at different activities afterwards. It was the usual weekend deal; the timing required military precision.

Another of my daughter's friends had also been invited, and as I buzzed around checking that each child had the clothes, money and items needed for their evening, I had a bright idea. The girl's mother was my good friend. She would be dropping her daughter off and I would see her for a few minutes. I wanted to give her a present and here was my chance. The present was a large tub of plants, so it had to be given when she was going straight home.

The tub contained seven healthy, good-sized impatiens that I had carefully nurtured from cuttings. I was so proud of myself. Not being much of a gardener, my success with these impatiens had raised my self-image considerably. Several times a week I'd admired the budding plants, praying for my friend and savouring the pleasure they would give her.

The day had come to give the gift. Much depended on being at the rendezvous on time. I started working on my youngest dreamer well before zero hour. I gave her regular countdowns on time remaining to departure. I prompted on what needed to be done and when. I helped where I could.

When it was time to go she was still in the shower. In spite of all my efforts, she wasn't ready. The rest of us sat in the car waiting. My whole body was tense and my mind circled compulsively around teenage selfishness and the futility of my efforts.

When she appeared, I roared off in the car, berating her for her repeated disregard for me and my instructions.

At the first corner, the tub of impatiens rolled over and potting mix was strewn across the back of the station wagon. I was steamed up inside, hating the pressure of modern life, Friday afternoon traffic and the thoughtlessness of children! I felt hard done by and frustrated, and also ashamed of myself for being so steamed up over so little.

On arriving at our friends' house, we discovered they weren't ready to leave. They'd tried to call to offer a pickup on the way, saving me a trip. The other girl wasn't even there—she was being picked up on the way.

Depositing my daughter, I drove around the corner and stopped. Why was I so upset inside? I apologised to the other children for over-reacting and we all prayed. Only then did the knot in my stomach start unravelling. When God wants to deal with something in us he often lets it come to a head in an exaggerated way. He likes to get it out into the open. He did something in me that day. My daughter has to change, of course, but that's another matter.

She has been improving since. But things don't have to go according to my schedule.

It took a while to clean up the mess in the back of the car. I felt so sad—three of the plants were broken. God spoke to me through those broken plants. My stress spoils and breaks things that are precious. I repotted them and decided to delay the gift in the hope that they would resprout.

I asked God to re-sprout them as a sign of his redemptive power in the whole matter. And he did! Several weeks later my friend was delighted to receive the tub, complete with all seven plants.

RUNNING ON EMPTY

⁓

*T*hroughout my childhood, we enjoyed regular visits from various uncles and aunties. These were great times.

One of my favourite uncles was a pastor. He had the clear, bright eyes of an earnest man, and I respected him deeply. I have never forgotten a true story he once told me. He was staying on the west coast of South Australia. One night, driving home from a meeting in a nearby town, he ran out of petrol far from any townships or services.

It was a dark night, and as he got out of his car, my uncle reflected that he had not seen another vehicle for a long time. At that moment, a car approached. It pulled up behind him, and a man got out. To my uncle's astonishment, the man greeted him by name and announced, "I've brought the petrol." Handing him a can of petrol, he got back into his car and drove away.

My uncle had never met the man before and never saw him again. He was sure he had encountered an angel.

God met his need in a concrete way when he was literally running on empty. Many times, when I've felt I'm running on empty, God has provided what was necessary for me to continue, too—maybe not as dramatically as he did for my uncle.

One such occasion came during my second pregnancy. It was a stressful time. We were remodelling our kitchen and bathroom with a one-year-old racing around, and I felt so ill. Although I had agreed to speak at a weekend women's retreat, I was not confident I could even drive myself there. Nevertheless, I knew it was God's will for me to do it.

The weekend proved so memorable, it's still fresh years later. My strength didn't extend to standing—I had to sit while I spoke. But God was present by his Spirit. He made good the resources I lacked. Rather than being limited by my weakness, it became an opportunity for him to display his strength in an unmistakable fashion.

Jesus often experienced the same thing. An outstanding case is his encounter with the Samaritan woman. According to John 4:6, Jesus sat down by the well, weary from his journey. It was the middle of the day, so he was undoubtedly hot and, probably, hungry. The disciples had gone to the nearby town to buy food.

Humanly speaking, Jesus was running on empty. Yet, after his remarkable interaction with the woman, he was refreshed and renewed. Upon their return, the disciples remarked with surprise, "Could someone have brought him food?" Doing his Father's will had brought its own refreshing.

Nevertheless, God doesn't intend us to stagger from challenge to challenge, constantly needing miraculous intervention to meet the demands of the day. We trust our wellbeing to God (as we trust our financial needs and safety to him)—but we still need to be responsible stewards of our energies.

Would you begin a journey without filling your petrol tank? A long trip may require refills. Petrol companies know this and have provided a network of stations across Australia. Is God less considerate?

The times when you're extended need to be balanced with times of replenishment. Jesus understood this; he made time for solitude with his Father among the constant demands of his ministry.

In February 1993, I felt so empty I didn't want to face the year ahead. I knew, from years of experience, that I could simply plod on and do, in God's grace, what had to be done. But my husband sent me away, telling me, "Take three days and go. Be by yourself with the Lord." Those three days of solitude did more good than I could have imagined.

Although it got me going again, I needed more. For years I had been asking the Lord for a major break from our responsibilities. At times, my spirit ached for replenishment, despite God's daily provision of power for what he had called us to do. Eventually I wondered if I should get my head out of the clouds and stop dreaming.

However, as I write, I sit with my family in our home in California. God has granted me a year with extra time to listen to him, and there's more to come.

Is this a useful model? God may not send you across the world for refreshment, but he may intend something more concrete than you expect. Renewal comes through quietness and rest, as well as obedient activity (Isaiah 40:31).

NEVER SATISFIED

⁂

hile sitting in a playground, waiting for my children, I overheard a conversation that made me smile.

"Don't keep pulling at your hair like that, darling."

"But Mummy, 1 don't like my hair."

"Why ever not? It's lovely hair."

"No, I don't like it. It's so curly and it always goes up. I want long hair like Kelly's."

"But darling, lots of girls wish they had curls like you. Grown-ups pay money to make their hair curly."

"I don't care, Mummy", she said, stamping her foot. "I only like my hair when 1 have a bath. Then it's long down my back. I want hair like Kelly's."

I remembered my own absolutely gorgeous niece saying the same thing at age three while the family smiled at her shining brown eyes and beautiful curls. Then my mind wandered to various grown-up friends.

Some friends of mine move house regularly. "I couldn't resist the light, airy kitchen in our new house. Ever since we'd moved into the previous place, I'd felt flat in the mornings; stumbling into that dark, dingy kitchen at the start of the day."

Six months later, the same friend passed her free time looking wistfully at real estate guides. She was frustrated with the size of the backyard. Houses with sweeps of lawn and shrubs on drip systems called to her. I'm not sure what the kitchen was like in the next house they owned, but the garden was lovely.

Such a lot of energy gets diverted into this restless process. Has the function of a comfortable, pleasant layout in your house become irritating through familiarity? In the attractive glow of a friend's new decor, my perfectly suitable family room pales into a most unsatisfactory mediocrity. What about the comfortable, functional parts of your marriage? In the excitement of a friend's trip to Hawaii won by her husband at work, your husband's faithful provision and steady kindness may taste like soup without salt.

Tastes and lifestyle factors change with the seasons of life. We make poor judgments sometimes about what we want or need—so of course adjustments have to be made. That's all part of living. But restlessness doesn't have to be.

Restlessness leads a circuitous route through life. We may progress, but it's with many loops and circles along the way. Sometimes it feels like nothing but circles. This is especially true if restless activity comes from unhappiness and dissatisfaction. Certainly, God stirs us up, sometimes, when something is wrong. He pokes and prods to get a message through. Dissatisfaction comes to a head and is resolved by a glorious new direction in life.

It's not these occasional crises to which I refer. Rather, it is to a pattern, over years, of never being satisfied. Julia came to peace about her home fairly easily—but kept dwelling on the limitations of her husband. She wished he would take more initiative emotionally. Her restlessness was expressed through redoing her garden regularly. She also subscribed to a number of magazines and kept trying to get her husband enrolled in courses on communication.

Anne, her friend, envied Julia's stable marriage. She would have swapped her fabulous home and garden for a husband who wasn't volatile and hot-tempered, any day. Anne took one course after another and started several small businesses. Some succeeded, but always, after a while, she lost interest.

For Christians, the process is often the same. It may be about jobs, homes or families, about spiritual gifts and opportunities. One church seems exciting, for a while, but doesn't offer challenge or opportunity to grow, in the longer term. Another offers plenty of opportunity to grow through service but no affirmation or support. Maybe the people aren't friendly or maybe too friendly for comfort! Are you satisfied with the gifts and ministry opportunities God has given you?

Perhaps your children are hard to handle. Maybe the work that fills each day seems insignificant. These are signals, prompting us to chase after God more energetically. Dissatisfaction often comes from somewhere deep inside. If I don't think God has a worthwhile job for me to do, I get caught in busy cycles about plants or houses or clothes. There's nothing wrong with these things, but a schedule driven by restless dissatisfaction feels and is wrong.

God does have worthwhile tasks for us to do. There's a promise in Ephesians 2:10. Busyness can never satisfy our need to engage with his eternal purposes.

Jesus made bold statements about satisfaction. To the outcast Samaritan woman in John 4:14, he said, "those who drink the water I give them will never thirst". Again, in John 6:35, he said, "I am the bread of life. Whoever comes to me will never go hungry." Dissatisfaction jolts us to find ourselves more deeply in Jesus.

Get off the frenzied loop. Be still for a while. Eat and drink him.

GREAT EXPECTATIONS

*lue skies above, gentle breeze blowing in my face. At Linden Park Primary School the end of the athletics day mile race beckoned at last. Rounding the last curve on the oval, I knew I was about to die—my legs just wouldn't go any further. Yet catching sight of the finishing line I actually managed to pick up speed. Somehow those fat little legs found more when hope of finishing the race kicked in.

Have you noticed how proximity to the toilet affects your bladder in the mornings? Stumbling in the right direction, keeping yourself together—then the prospect of relief and suddenly it's get there quickly or burst. While you have to hold on you can. When you almost don't have to you almost can't.

Sometimes the sight of the goal spurs me on. Other times it makes things harder. What I'm expecting matters every step of the way. How I'm feeling is constantly influenced by how the present compares with what I thought it would be like by now.

Same deal when it comes to walking with Jesus and seeing him transform our lives. We live in tension, in the age of the now and the not yet. We are safe, heading for glory, but not there yet. At any time the Spirit can break through and completely change someone, yet it has been two thousand years since Jesus left, promising to come back. Generations have lived and died with little dramatic intervention from the Spirit. Other generations have seen him do incredible things. Some are seeing it right now in various parts of the world.

How do we set our expectations? It's silly to say that we shouldn't have them. We read the Bible and see the promises; of course we're supposed to expect things of God. Just as he wants us to know what he expects of us.

My father rejected the gospel in his youth and remained hard towards Jesus in spite of divine overtures towards him over decades. One of his closest friends, his brother-in-law, was a pastor who died without seeing Dad change his attitude to Jesus. After my mother was converted she had 14 years of marriage with constant struggle over her church involvement and no suggestion of answers to her daily prayers for her husband.

In such a situation it is easy to get discouraged, to think God's promises aren't true. At least to wonder if there's something wrong with you. Life doesn't meet your expectations. If the Bible were true, then the prayer of a faithful wife would be answered (and of sisters, friends and eventually a daughter). Anything you ask in Jesus' name would happen. Wouldn't it?

Fourteen years is a long time to struggle, watching children grow up with tensions that God doesn't desire as ideal. Years of self-doubt, of frustration, of discouragement for those expecting God to act. The more specific the expectations the more potential for attack and discouragement.

Dad's story had a wonderful ending, at least from the eternal perspective. He died after a gruelling battle with cancer. Emaciated by two years of sickness and pain, he had been reconciled with God. That's another story in itself. But God did act. He fulfilled his promises. He chose the method and the timing.

God's commitment to us is unwavering. He's in it for the long haul. We find it hard to set our sights at the right distance and so our expectations keep tripping us up. God acts and catches me by surprise because I'd settled into a non-expectant mode to protect myself from disappointment. Or I get all excited about something I think he's going to do and crash-land when week after week fails to produce what I was expecting.

Do many scriptures make promises about timing? I can't think of any offhand. God guarantees his character and his goals, not the details of how and when.

We signed up for a race that turns out to be a marathon, not a sprint. If we don't keep poring over the guide book and communicating with the coach, we'll trip up on some surprising terrain. Each kilometre brings different challenges and must be tackled differently. No simplistic formula will get us through every part of the course with our sights set appropriately. Only the coach can do that.

THE SCREEN AND THE MIRROR

(FOR BLYTHE)

Two hospital beds side by side,
shielded from each other by a drab screen,
white and grey, as befits the place.

On one my dying mother,
white and grey as befits her,
lying on the threshold of death.

How wrinkled and pasty and insubstantial she looks!
All that life reduced to this small form,
a bundle barely alive.

On the other bed my baby daughter,
so full of life,
yet tiny, scarcely arrived.

I bundled her in a soft white blanket
and placed her in the middle of the vacant bed,
so as to wash my hands and stroke my mother.

My back to both, I glance up
and there in the mirror see these two,

side by side, yet screened from one another.

Two small white bundles
poised on the brink of eternity
and me.

Death and life
Past and future
Separated by a hospital screen
but intersecting in me.

To the left as I gaze at the mirror, I see my mother leaving.
I see all the ages of womanhood stretching back to Eve.

To the right, my daughter,
and all the women to come.

They are not separated really.
The screen is flimsy.
The mirror more true.

Oh, Lord, thank you for placing me
at this point in your history.
Thank you for my spot in the great procession
of women towards glory.

Thank you for my mother ...
... receive her.
Thank you for my daughter ...
... fill her even now.
Thank you for my life ...
Oh, dear Father,
live in me
live me
let me live in you
now and forever.

THE LOVE EXCHANGE

Our 16-year-old son came home with a lip ring a few days ago. We were upset because we'd told him piercings had to wait until he was 18. He really, Really, REALLY wanted one and he'd decided that a fait accompli was more promising than discussion.

Where does loving meet controlling? Guiding become intruding? Respect, relationship, tolerance of difference—these swirl about a household with breathtaking fluidity during the teenage years.

The three of us had a big talk. It wasn't easy. Sixteen isn't 13 and a lip ring isn't a tattoo. But there needs to be communication. Respect and communication remain hugely important at every age.

From our point of view we've not batted an eyelid at sagging pants and hair dyed black and blonde. We're remarkably relaxed parents! From his point of view we're over-the-top strict and uptight. The age-old push and pull, the progression from one generation to the next rolls on as it has through history. We want to guide our children. We want them to hear and receive us. They want to have their impact on us, to make a difference, to be different, to find themselves freely.

Our son's disregard of our wishes presented us with a dilemma. There are many areas in which we are not prepared to bend, and in the important things he has so far accepted our boundaries. Should we soften our stance on this issue? If not, there would need to be consequences.

The lip ring is still in—for now. It's school holidays, anyway. After our talk, though, we would be very unimpressed if presented with a new fait accompli contrary to our expressed wishes. If he really Really REALLY wants something, he's going to need to talk to us.

Love, guidance and control get quite mixed up between parents and children. We're all so far from perfect. We bring our weaknesses, faults, pride and needs to the exchange, both parents and children.

Between God and us, his children, guidance, control and love are biggies, too. How does he approach guiding us in our formation? He doesn't bring weakness and faults to the process as we do.

For some time now I have found great power in a simple prayer: "Father, I give you permission to work in me however you choose." It has been so liberating. Rarely does a day go by without me praying this out loud.

Well, recently I was walking the dog as usual in the morning. Morning light filtered softly through the trees as I rounded the agapanthus corner. "Father, do as you want in me today. I give you permission. I invite you in."

Suddenly I sensed such a presence of God with me. No physical sensations or visions, but a sense of his tangible presence. It was as if he was ahead, moving towards me with arms outstretched for an embrace. His response filled my mind in an instant: "Just let me love you. Receive my love."

It was as if he was pressing in on me, just wanting to gush, to overwhelm, to deluge me with love. Joy, warmth, abandonment. It took my breath away.

Yet even in that instant I could sense the strength of his presence. His love flowing into me would be strong and do work. Like molten lava, the flow would forge new pathways, push things out of the way, reshape the landscape of my inner world.

Inviting him to work in me was the same as receiving his love, receiving him. He was like a husband overcome with delight and eager to press his love on me. Yet like a huge force, undeniable, unstoppable, with all the answers and the power to deliver.

How amazing is God? I felt no fear, no caution, no doubt. Only his delight and my delight. How I wanted him to get all the work and all the changing done, so there would be no hindrance to the love exchange between us.

Not bad for a short morning walk. And then I returned to the dishes, the phone calls and the washing.

Guidance, control, refining—such heavy words. And they are heavy. They're important. Yet they are only a gateway. God's all about love, really. Being with him is more like embracing and singing, like dancing with flowers in your hair, twirling and laughing, than about suffering and being refined.

The arguments and tension and tears, the nappies, the red lights, the pain and disappointment, the car breakdowns and money worries and tiredness. Yes, and the lip rings, too. They're all just the path we walk to the love exchange.

FOR MORE INFORMATION

For more information about Merilyn, please visit her website at
https://www.ozpacker.com/merilynpacker
or write to

Luminant Publications
PO Box 305
Greenacres SA 5085
Australia

www.ingramcontent.com/pod-product-compliance
Lightning Source LLC
Chambersburg PA
CBHW072118020426
42334CB00018B/1639